Center for Basque Studies
Basque Diaspora and Migration Studies Series, No. 6

Buffalotarrak

Edited by

Dollie Iberlin and David Romtvedt

Revised

With a new introduction by David Romtvedt

Basque Diaspora and Migration Studies Series, No. 6

Center for Basque Studies
University of Nevada, Reno
Reno, Nevada

N

This book was published with generous financial support from the Basque Goverment.

Basque Diaspora and Migration Studies Series, No. 6

Center for Basque Studies
University of Nevada, Reno
Reno, Nevada 89557
http://basque.unr.edu

Cover and series design © 2011 by Jose Luis Agote.
Cover photograph: Courtesy of the Johnson County Library Basque Photos collection. Pelota game in the 1930s played on the side of John Esponda's barn near Buffalo, Wyoming.

Buffalotarrak was first published by Red Hills Publications in association with the Ucross Foundation.

Grateful acknowledgment is made to the following for permission to reprint previously published material:

Joseph P. Castelli, Desert Research Institute Publications on the Social Sciences, and the Basque Studies Program at the University of Nevada for edited excerpts from Mr. Castelli's essay "The Basque Community in Buffalo, Wyoming," which appeared in *Anglo-American Contributions to Basque Studies: Essays in Honor of Jon Bilbao,* edited by William A. Douglass, Richard W. Etulain, and William H. Jacobsen, Jr., copyright © 1977 by Joseph P. Castelli and the Desert Research Institute.

Dollie Iberlin for "Powder River to the Big Horns," which is an edited excerpt from *The Basque Web,* copyright© 1981 by Dollie Iberlin.

David Romtvedt and White Pine Press for "1989: Buffalo: Aitatxi, Grandfather, A Weed;" and "1920: Buffalo: Amatxi, Grandmother, the Dignity of Work," which appeared in *Crossing Wyoming,* copyright © 1992, 1993 by David Romtvedt.

Frances Beckner Thompson and *The Denver Post* for "Wyoming's 'Mother of the Basques,'" which appeared in *The Denver Post's Empire Magazine* for April 13, 1969; Frances Beckner Thompson, *The Wool Sack* and *The Buffalo Bulletin* for "Against All Odds."

Historical photographs in *Buffalotarrak* are from the Johnson County, Wyoming Library's Basque photography collection, and are printed with permission of the Local History Department of the Johnson County Library.

Photographs from the 2011 Buffalo NABO festival are courtesy of *The Buffalo Bulletin* and photographer Tom Milsted.

Thank you also to Simon Iberlin, to the staff of the Johnson County Library, local historian Patty Myers , and to the Ucross Foundation for their support of this project.

Buffalo Basque community group photo at St. John the Baptist Catholic Church, Buffalo, Wyoming, late 1960s. Source: Johnson County Library, Basque Photos collection.

Contents

Buffalo, Wyoming and *Buffalotarrak*:
    Introduction to the Second Edition 13
    David Romtvedt

Jeanne Marie Etchemendy 33
    The Ones Who Stand Up 35

Joseph P. Castelli 39
    The Basques of Buffalo, Wyoming 41

Kathleen Michelena Smith 49
    Visiting My Family Home 51

David Romtvedt 57
    Basque Music and Wyoming 59
    1920: Buffalo: Amatxi, Grandmother, the Dignity of Work ... 65
    1989: Buffalo: Aitatxi, Grandfather, a Weed 67
    With Simon at Four Mile Ranch 71

Dollie Iberlin 85
    Powder River to the Big Horns 87
    A Sheepman 95

Frances Beckner Thompson 101
    Against All Odds 103
    Wyoming's Mother of the Basques 107

Buffalotarrak is dedicated to these Basque families

Amestoy
Auzqui
Bidonde
Bejino
Bordarrampe
Camino
Carricaburu
Cinquambre
Curuchet
Curutchet
Escoz
Errecart
Esponda
Etchemendy
Falxa
Garro
Goni
Harriet
Hasquet
Ibarra
Iberlin
Inchauspe
Indart

Iriberry
Irigaray
Juanicotena
Larralde
Martirena
Marton
Maya
Michelena
Petrau
Pradere
Reculusa
Rodriguez
Taberna
Urruty
Vasco

Skaters on Clear Creek with Big Horn Mountains to the west, Buffalo, Wyoming, early twentieth century. Source: Johnson County Library, Basque Photos collection.

Buffalo, Wyoming and *Buffalotarrak*:
Introduction to the Second Edition

When I came to Buffalo, Wyoming in late October, 1984, my intention was to spend two months at the Ucross Foundation—an artists' colony for writers, composers, and visual artists—and then return unscathed to my life on the Olympic Peninsula. Shortly after I got to Ucross, I met a local potter named Margo Brown. We had dinner together, we went to the movies, we went dancing. I started wondering about my plans.

I was falling in love with Margo and through her with the Basque people of Buffalo and with the Basque people's history. It is a history governed not so much by chronology as by association. And in the recounting of the associations, meaning lies not so much in the memory of particular events as in the mapping of movement forward and backward into what has been romantically labeled the "mists of time." Time past and time future.

The cautious say that the Basques arrived in their current homeland along the shores of the Bay of Biscay and in the Pyrenees Mountains perhaps four thousand years ago, but maybe, they allow, it was six thousand years ago. Or it could have been eight. Perhaps the people who became Basque are the ones who produced the famous cave paintings found in southwestern Europe, paintings such as those at Altamira and Lascaux and Chauvet. These scenes depict mostly large animals—bison, deer, horses—along with tracings of the human hand. In one recently discovered cave, there is a large painting of a sea bream, a great delicacy in Basque cuisine. The cave images were made between ten and thirty-five thousand years ago and so maybe the Basques have been around that long. A bird bone flute has been dated as twenty-seven thousand years old and is of the same design as that of the currently used Basque three-holed *txistu*. Along with the *txalaparta* and the *alboka*, the *txistu* is among the most ancient of Basque musical instruments and so maybe the Basques have been around for just as long, playing music, making paintings, eating seafood.

The Basques tell us that the Garden of Eden was in the Basque Country and that Basque was the original tongue given to us by God. We all spoke Basque until the fatal day when human hubris shown in the construction of the tower of Babel—a tower with which humans meant to climb to Heaven—so enraged the Lord that he confounded our tongues. Now we have thousands of languages and the onomato-poetic word babble.

At Ucross, the fall of 1984 was dominated by snow and brilliant sun-filled days. I often ate my lunch beside the creek, the water running cold between snowy banks, then turning to ice as fall's cold solidified. I'd take two coats, one to wear and one to throw down on the snow where I sat. I'd lean on my elbow and look at the surrounding hills, the snow and the wind scoured expanses of rock.

One night I borrowed a van belonging to the foundation so that I could drive to Buffalo to visit Margo. I made two drinks and set the glasses on the dashboard. Somehow I thought it would be romantic to show up with cocktails. But the van's heater and defroster didn't work and I had to keep scraping the window to see where I was going. I forgot about the drinks and by the time I got to Buffalo, they, like the creek at Ucross, were turning to ice.

After I left Ucross, I came back to Wyoming often to see Margo. As I got to know her, I got to know her family, the great interlocking community of people who had immigrated to Buffalo from Iparralde—the northern part of the Basque Country—in the first third of the twentieth century. There were brothers and sisters, cousins, nieces and nephews. Many came from Arnegi, up the river Nives from Donibane Garazi, the capital of the province of Nafarroa Beherea. Others came from nearby villages—Luzaide, Esterenzubi, Baigorri, and Banka. Sometimes I would go to Sunday dinner with Margo's family. There would be ten or twenty or even thirty people at these dinners, all related to each other. People asked me who I was, where I came from, who my family was. I was both uncomfortable with and attracted to the closeness of their lives, the sense of being members of a clan. It was something I'd never experienced in my own family.

It was in the late spring of 1986 that Jeanne Marie Etchemendy, née Ansolabehere known to most of the local Basques simply as Aunt Jane, summoned me to an audience at her home. Summoned and audience are the words that fit given Aunt Jane's place in the Basque community. I knew that Aunt Jane's husband Pierre Etche-mendy, known as Pete, was related to Margo's grandfather John Iber-lin. I asked Margo's mother Dollie Iberlin (who served as coeditor of this book) about the connection and learned that John had married Pete's sister Jeanne so Aunt Jane was Margo's great aunt. Pete and Jeanne's sister Catherine had married Peter Harriet so the Har-riets were Aunt Jane's inlaws, nieces, and nephews as well as Margo's aunts, uncles, and cousins. There were also relationships by marriage with Caminos, Espondas, and another branch of the Etchemendy family. Years later, I said to Margo's aunt Madeline Harriet (who was the daughter of an Etchemendy and an Iberlin) that it seemed she was related to every Basque in town. "Not every one," she said, with a little growl and I wondered which of her Basque neighbors she was glad not to be related to.

The family relationships weren't clear to me but the visit to Aunt Jane was—I was taking a test and I didn't know what the test was to cover or how I would be scored. In that sense it was like most tests. Walking up the steps to Aunt Jane's house, I felt like Dorothy and her companions—the Scarecrow, The Tin Woodsman, and the Cowardly Lion—as they walked down the long Emerald City Hallway to the chamber of the Great and Powerful Oz.

From the mid-nineteenth to the mid-twentieth century, non-Basque people in the American West came to think of Basques as an exotic and deeply foreign bunch. While Basques often spoke several languages—most commonly French and Spanish in addition to their native Euskara—English was little known to them and so the

English-speaking Americans often found it easier to deal with their Basque neighbors by picking a single prominent man who spoke English and treating this man as a sort of ambassador from afar. In many of the ranching communities of the inter-American West, the ambassador was known as the King of the Basques.

In Buffalo, the first king was John Esponda and on his death in 1936, the crown passed to John Camino. But by the time of my arrival, Basques were in many ways like their neighbors. The first generation of American-born Basques had attended the public schools. If, like my future father-in-law Simon Iberlin, they spoke no English when starting school, they were mocked mercilessly. Simon would tell me many times that the first English he learned was "Simple Simon," the name he was called by his classmates. Only six years old, Simon was ashamed and vowed that he would learn English quickly. He would fit in. He would not be called Simple Simon.

When they finished school, many of these American-born Basques married non-Basques. The children of such marriages almost always grew up speaking only English at home and so that ancient pillar of Basquesness—the Basque language—began to erode. Since their conversion to Christianity between the years 900 and 1200 c.e., Basques had become staunchly and nearly universally Catholic. Marriage outside the Basque community often meant that one partner in the marriage was Catholic and the other Protestant and so the strength of the church as a marker of Basqueness also began to erode. Even sport was influenced with the young Basque-American boys playing football and basketball more often than the handball games that were a central part of life in every European Basque village.

The kings had faded away and now there was Aunt Jane, the matriarch of the Buffalo Basques. If Aunt Jane was a Basque Queen replacing the now unnecessary Basque Kings, I was a foreign knave. At the time a graduate student in folklore and ethnomusicology, my scholarly field of interest was in the Caribbean musics that reflect the intermingling of European and African musics in the Americas. But my personal interest in seeing Margo led me to suddenly discover that I had a powerful interest in the music of the Basque diasporic community in Buffalo.

Scholars have noted that the most striking thing about Basque music is that it reflects what most European musics must have sounded like centuries before. Largely untouched by African influences, the Basques have maintained what some outsiders have described as a living museum of European musical concepts and practices. I know living museum is an oxymoron but the idea is enticing—a music happily existing outside its time. To the Basques, of course, there was no museum, only music.

I designed a project investigating the place of traditional dance and music in Buffalo's Basque community. I would do a series of interviews, attend Basque events, study Basque style button accordion, write an article on the subject, and hang around with Margo. But before I could start, I needed some general knowledge about the Basques.

The first thing I learned was that most Basques immigrants to the American West arrived late in the period of European settlement. These latecomers took the jobs that were left and that required little or no English—generally sheepherding. They spent much of the year far from town living alone talking to their dogs, the sheep, and the sky and trees.

Before they came to America, the Basques had, for thousands of years, occupied a small well-defined region of southwestern Europe. They had been invaded repeatedly by outsiders with dreams of imperial grandeur—the Celts who sought plunder, the Romans who bore first Hellenism and later Christianity, the armies of the Middle East and North Africa who replaced Christianity with Islam, and finally the French and the Castilians who dragged in their wake the modern nation state. The Basques had survived all these invasions, partly by playing one force against another and partly by keeping to themselves. A mythology grew up around them—they were a clannish, strange, private, and fierce people. It didn't hurt that their language, the only non Indo-European language in Europe, was said to be incomprehensible. If you want to be left alone, strangeness will serve you well.

I can't remember how Aunt Jane issued her invitation to me. I imagined that she wanted to find out what my intentions were toward Margo but years later Margo said Aunt Jane never kept such close tabs on her, in fact never paid her much mind at all.

"We used to go to her place at Christmas where we had to stand in place for the living Nativity scene. Somebody was Joseph and somebody was Mary or you could be one of the visiting kings. That's about all. Aunt Jane might not even have known you were seeing me. I bet she wanted to see you because you were an intellectual, a person who read books. She read books."

That brought back something I'd forgotten—when Aunt Jane first spoke to me, it was in English. Later, when she learned that I spoke French, she switched to that language and I found that in French she was another person. In French, she lived in the world of ideas and concepts. She was speculative and meditative. In English, she'd been only practical, speaking of the weather, of lambing and shearing, of cooking and cleaning, of work. I wondered what she was like in Basque.

It was one of the first really warm spring days. I'd ridden up to the house and leaned my bicycle against the white picket fence then begun the walk to the door. The house was a plain rectangle. Painted white, it had a steep roof covered in t-lock shingles. There was no porch, just a concrete stoop leading to the front door at the gable end facing the street.

When I knocked on the heavy wooden door, there was no answer so I knocked again. The door swung open and there I was, face to face with Aunt Jane. She looked at me for what seemed a long time but I saw it wasn't a threatening or disapproving look and felt relieved. She stepped to one side and said, "Come in."

Passing through the doorway, I was immediately in the living room. The windows were small and curtained so the room was dark even in the day. "Sit down." Aunt Jane said, "I will get you some lemonade. Do you want lemonade? I'll be right back."

"Yes, lemonade, that would be fine."

She turned and disappeared through a doorway.

I looked around and only then noticed that the room was lined with bookshelves. Most of the Basques in Buffalo had come from small farming communities. They'd had little opportunity to go to school and so it was rare to see many books in their houses. But here was a room in which there was almost nothing but books. I walked along the rows of shelves and saw titles in French, Basque, Spanish, and English. On one end of the room was a large overstuffed chair where a person might spend many hours with book after book.

I wandered along, now and again taking a volume from a shelf and glancing through it. From the kitchen, I could hear the sound of a knife on a cutting board. "Do you need any help?" I called.

"No. I'm just cutting up the lemons then I'll squeeze them. You have to squeeze hard to get all the juice out. They're stubborn."

In a few more minutes Aunt Jane appeared with two tall narrow glasses on a small tray. She offered me a glass, took one herself, set the tray down, and pointed me toward the large overstuffed chair. Sitting down I sank into a sea of cushions. Aunt Jane glided sideways into another chair. She was tall and sturdy and did not sink into her chair.

I still figured her main idea was to find out about my intentions concerning Margo but she said nothing about the family, speaking instead about Buffalo and her arrival there from Baigorri.

"My family made sure I went to school." She said, "But the school was in French. Only at the church could you learn in Basque. When I finished school, I worked as a private tutor, planning to get a job as a regular schoolteacher. Even after I left school I kept trying to learn and to think. I was happy teaching and wouldn't have left home but for Hitler. I had worked in the Spanish Basque Country until the violence of the Civil War there made it impossible to stay. After that, I worked in Angoulême, France. In those days, it was unusual for an unmarried Basque woman to live and work away from home. Most young people stayed with their parents until they were married and then the couple often moved in with the husband's parents. My mother and father worried about me living away from home. If

Hitler and the Nazis occupied France, then it would be safer for me to leave Europe altogether.

"Everyone knew what the Nazis had done to help Franco and the fascists during the Civil War. They bombed Gernika which was nothing more than a market town for surrounding farms. It was late afternoon and there were farmers selling their produce, mothers shopping, children running around, old people talking. You could see the pilots' eyes when they flew down to drop the bombs. They came that close. Now the Nazis were attacking all of Europe. Whatever was to come, it was going to be terrible. That's what my parents believed and so they had me leave.

"Maybe I should have stayed. Many people in the Basque Country were able to help during the war. A lot of people made their living by taking goods back and forth across the border to sell. The French and Spanish governments called it smuggling. But why should Basques pay French and Spanish taxes for taking goods from one Basque village to another?

"Many men and women knew the secret paths through the mountains, tiny passes and twisting routes no one would find. There were places where if you took a wrong step in the dark, you might fall down a long slope so it would be hard for someone who didn't know the local mountains. As the war went on, more and more Allied pilots were shot down. There was a system of helping get those downed pilots across the Pyrenees and to the coast where they could be put on boats back to England. Franco's Spain was officially neutral but it supported the Nazis so you had to be careful even once you were over the Pyrenees. The people who guided the pilots over the border were now heroes rather than smugglers."

I sipped my lemonade.

"Do you like it?"

"Yes."

Aunt Jane changed the subject to Wyoming. "When I first came here, I was very lonely and unhappy. It was so different from the Basque Country. There it is green and the hills are close and continuous and the sea is never too far away. The rains come regularly and for many months of the year it is overcast and gray but never so cold. You can grow many kinds of vegetables and fruits.

"Here it was awful—the winter was so cold and then in summer it was as hot as the African desert. Months might go by with almost no rain and the grasses would dry and burn. Then the sheep and cattle suffered. But one thing I liked right from the start was the sky. I'd never seen a sky like Wyoming's—so blue, and it is a blue that doesn't exist in the Basque Country, wide and deep as if the sky will go on forever. As time went by, my love for the sky came to make me love other things in Wyoming. Do you like it here?"

"Yes, well, there are things, I . . ."

She waved her hand as if waving away explanations. "I think maybe it was the same for me. But I came to understand it and back then, although Buffalo was a much smaller town, it was more alive. You could feel the energy of it, the movement. There was no television and no concerts and only a few places where a person could go out to eat a meal so people spent a lot of time with each other, eating and dancing and drinking wine and talking—talk, talk, talking. People could talk."

She told me about a man who every year ordered a railroad car of red grapes from California. "The railroad came to Buffalo then." She explained. "Later they changed the line so that it went north to Sheridan and bypassed Buffalo. Then there were neither passenger nor freight trains coming here and there still aren't. Now there are no passenger trains in all of Wyoming." She paused and leaned back in her chair.

"More lemonade?"

"No, I'm fine. Thank you."

"You should stay in Buffalo." She advised me. "Young people who are raised here don't stay and no new young people move here. The town will die without young people. If you stay, you can help it be alive. Maybe you need a girlfriend."

I wondered if she was suggesting it was alright for me to court Margo.

"Yes, Buffalo was smaller but more alive then. The shops were busy and now there are almost no shops. You can't buy underwear here. Did you know that?"

"No." Underwear seemed a strange subject given her suggestion that I needed a girlfriend.

"Well, it's true. You have to go to Sheridan thirty-six miles away to buy underwear. We need young people to come here and help keep the place young and energetic. You are studying Basque people, is that right?"

"Well, I'm interviewing people, mostly the ones who've started the local Basque dance group, like Mary Juanicotena. She went to California thinking she'd never come back and while she was there she got involved with a dance group and saw how dancing was helping to keep the Basque community together. She decided to come home and start a dance group here. And I'm talking to Florence Camino and Jean Cinquambre who play accordion for the group. Jean Cinquambre lost the thumb on his right hand. Got it caught in the power take off of a tractor but he still plays the big chromatic accordion and does well even without his thumb."

Aunt Jane nodded and smiled again then asked, "Do you know the story of the Devil coming to the Basque Country to convert the people?"

I shook my head no.

"The Devil had no luck because he couldn't speak Basque so he decided he would learn the language and then he could convert people to sin. He studied for seven years and at the end all he could say was *bai* and *ez*—yes and no—which wasn't enough to convert anyone so he gave up in disgust and went to France and Spain where the languages are easier to learn, the people are easier to tempt, and sin is more ordinary."

I laughed.

"You shouldn't laugh. The French and Spanish are more easily tempted. But to tempt anyone, you need to know the language. Even if you are not so interested in temptation, it's important to speak to people. You, for example, need to learn Basque and the best way for an outsider who is a young man to learn the language is to get a Basque girlfriend."

I was sure that Aunt Jane was aware that Margo knew only a few words in Basque.

"For you, it won't be like it was for the Devil. It will still take seven years but in the end you will speak Basque and you won't feel a need to convert anyone to sin as, with a girlfriend, you will be happy."

"Maybe if the Devil had a girlfriend, he wouldn't cause all the trouble he does."

Now Aunt Jane laughed. "Remember that it will take seven years but, more importantly, remember that the days don't count, only the nights."

That's what Aunt Jane told me on our first meeting—to learn Basque you must spend seven years with a Basque woman and only the nights count. She took my glass to the kitchen and then showed me to the door.

Some years later, when Margo and I were married, I was playing the button accordion for the Buffalo Basque dance troupe. In each local community, Basques throughout the American West have a yearly summer picnic. In the early days, these picnics were a way for herders to get together with each other and with friends and family from town. Townspeople would ride on horseback or in horse drawn wagons up the mountain. Later they drove. The local priest would say Mass, there'd be a dinner, people would play games—jump rope and tug-of-war, weightlifting and carrying—and there would be dancing to the music of the button accordion.

In Buffalo, the summer picnic has always been held on August fifteenth. This is the day on which the church celebrates the Assumption, the bodily taking up of Mary into heaven after her death. For me, the Assumption explains some of the strangeness of our lives on earth. How did we get here and who will take us home? We only know that through our associations we can be carried far beyond the limits of the body.

Some of that feeling permeates the August fifteenth picnic, a time when people tend to be a little sentimental about the past. Another year has made its round and we come together to celebrate, to take pleasure in each other's company.

Aunt Jane was at the picnic and, throughout the dancing, I could see her seated regally in a chair along one of the side walls of the building where the dancing was going on. When the dancers stopped for a break, I approached her. I'd now been in Buffalo for over seven years. I'd married Margo which made me Aunt Jane's great nephew by marriage.

"*Arratsalde on.*" I said. Good afternoon.

"*Arratsalde on. Nola zaude?*" She answered. Good afternoon. How are you?

"*Ondo. Eta zu?*" Fine, and you?

Aunt Jane said something I didn't understand and I apologized, explaining that though I knew a little more than the Devil, I still didn't really speak Basque. "But I am studying and hope that one day I will be more fluent."

"How are you studying?" She asked.

"I'm taking an extension course from the University of Nevada."

"You are studying Batua?" She asked.

"Yes, Batua."

Batu means united and *batua* means the united thing. Created after the death of Franco, Batua took elements from several dialects and used them to create a language that people in every village and province could share. The hope was and remains that with Batua we can increase the likelihood that Basque will not disappear from the earth. Newspaper and magazine articles are written in Batua. Radio and television and movies are made in Batua. Children learn Batua in school.

"Batua is not Basque." Aunt Jane said and a look of disgust came over her face.

"But it is what people are learning now and without it Basque may not survive."

"It's not Basque."

On this point there was no use arguing so I excused myself, explaining that it was time for me to play again for the dancers. When I walked away, Aunt Jane was still scowling.

*****

Many years have gone by and Jeanne Marie Etchemendy, née Ansolabehere—Aunt Jane—has died. I recount these two conversations with her both because I seek to honor her memory and because I think they reveal something of what endures for the Basque people in Buffalo—not so much artifacts and relics as ideas and sensibilities.

While Aunt Jane was a passionate spokesperson for Basque culture, she was not a preservationist and she gave little of her energy to worrying about what we have lost. She wanted Buffalo to be a vibrant place but that didn't mean we should do the same things we have always done. Having left her homeland, if not quite in flight, then certainly with the breath of Hitler behind her, she knew that all is change.

When she wrote her essay for this volume, she pointed out that while the Basques have been called the mystery people of Europe, they are not so mysterious to themselves. She was suggesting that we must be clearheaded and avoid romanticizing our lives, avoid falsifying our experience. She warned us not to have excessive pride in our distinctiveness. We are, after all, as distinctive as everyone else.

Aunt Jane's essay and those that accompanied it were originally written to celebrate the North American Basque Organization's (NABO) 1995 National meeting and festival held in Buffalo, Wyoming. The essayists were, in the main, not professional writers. They were local people whose stories could give us a feel for Basque life in Buffalo. The writers were sometimes shy about putting words down on paper but they were excited about their stories and eager to offer something of their experience.

It was personal. We see this in Kathleen Michelena Smith's story of going for the first time to her father's home in Gipuzkoa. The first time she saw the ocean and the boats in the bay. The first time she met her uncle and cousins. The difficulties of communicating—

somebody speaks only French, somebody else only Basque, a third person English and Spanish. Hugs and tears. A cup of *kafesnea* and anise liqueur.

We see the personal in Frances Beckner Thompson's admiration for the hardiness of the Basque people she knew—Catherine Marton and the herder Jean Auzqui, their reluctance to complain no matter how challenging their lives might be. Thompson describes Auzqui, who after a serious accident in winter and a heroic struggle to get help, was forced to spend nine weeks in a hospital bed. She tells us that Auzqui couldn't read, had no family, no interest in watching TV or listening to the radio, and had no hobbies. Yet ". . . he lay quietly. He had no need to keep busy and never seemed restless."

It was years later that Jean Auzqui died while working. His body lay in a pasture where he'd gone to check on a band of sheep. In the time since 1995, Frances Beckner Thompson has died, too, and yet both she and Jean Auzqui remain alive in the telling of Jean's story.

In addition to their personal tone, what strikes me now about these essays is their warmth. The writers were not studying and examining Basque history so much as revealing their relationships to and within the Basque community. Even Joseph P. Castelli, a non-Basque scholar and professor of cultural geography, expressed his connection to his "field of study" by ending his biographical note with the words "*Stay Basque.*" It was an unusually personal exhortation from someone doing an academic study. Was he worried?

Castelli tells us that, unlike many Basque communities, Buffalo lacked Basque markers that were present in other towns. The Basques never clustered in a single neighborhood and they never built their houses using the architectural models of the European Basque Country. There was never a separate Basque Church, nor a Basque restaurant or grocery. Aside from an informal wall for handball built at John Esponda's place in the early twentieth century there was never a *frontoi*—a handball court such as exists in every Basque village and which is often the physical and psychic center of the community.

Castelli explained that the single thing holding Basques together in Buffalo was the "ownership of land and the operation of sheep ranches on that land." There'd been the Idlewild Hotel which served as a boarding house for herders, and the 21 Club where Basque men went to socialize but both of those were closed by 1995. There was the Basque-owned KBBS radio station, which aired The Basque Hour, a weekly program of local news, information, and music in Basque but it wasn't too many years after Castelli wrote that it too was gone—sold to a media corporation. The Basque Hour was replaced by a computer generated music playlist linked to national marketing parameters.

It sounds like an elegy but Castelli wasn't so elegiac. He calmly noted that if there was to remain a Basque culture in Buffalo, its markers would be other than the Basque language and the sheep industry. Perhaps it was a kindly warning.

In 2011, young Basques in Buffalo, almost all of whom are of mixed heritage, go off to college and study to take up the same array of professions that non-Basque Americans pursue. Like young people throughout the country, when they finish college they often move far from home to start jobs and families.

So what is this thing called Basque in Buffalo, Wyoming? I think that it's a notion of community and an ease with a multifaceted identity. The Cajun fiddler Al Berard has said that he can be both a Cajun and an American. "I love boudin and chicory laced coffee and also Coca-Cola and a hamburger."

When Berard tries to explain being both American and Cajun, the metaphor he invokes is based on food. Food is an aspect of expressive culture and expressive culture is an essential component of identity—food, stories, clothing styles, songs, and dances. Some have suggested that the celebration of these things is acceptable because they are innocuous. They do not threaten the majority culture. I think this misses the point of what matters for it is just such apparently innocuous things that tell us who we are.

In 2006 and again in 2011, Buffalo was the host community, as it had been in 1988 and 1995 for NABO's yearly meeting and festival.

In 2006, about four thousand visitors came from around the country to the festival and in 2011 about six thousand attended the event. This is in a town of slightly under four thousand residents.

At the 2011 NABO festival, there was a parade to mark the beginning of the weekend of festivities. The local high school marching band—not known for presenting Basque music—played a traditional Basque tune that is the standard accompaniment for the local Basque dancers in parades. The dancers danced down the street, stopping at the bridge over Clear Creek where they performed a fandango and *arin* as Basques have done throughout Buffalo's history. Buffalo's community steel drum band—an ensemble that didn't exist until 2009 and which is also not known for presenting Basque music—played a Basque song from Bizkaia—"Domingo da Domeka"—in the parade.

Leading up to and during the weekend, Buffalo's main street was lined with red, white, and green Basque flags. Red and white geraniums in their sea of green leaves were planted in front of every store. The city hung more geraniums in baskets from the town's light poles. Local high school students volunteered to pick up trash in the park during festival events and a local golfer loaned his golf cart so that the kids could more easily pick the trash up. Some people complained that the kids were having too much fun on the golf cart.

Volunteers wrote newspaper articles and brochures describing Basque history in Buffalo. They designed and printed posters. A local band donated its sound system as did the high school and a local business—three sound systems. A crew of seven not only volunteered to run these sound systems but each sound crew member paid twenty dollars for the official sound crew t-shirt. It was black and had the Basque flag and the words "Gora Euskadi"—Up with the Basque Country—printed on it. Volunteers sold drinks and lamb burgers, and *lukainka* sausage and bread and cheese and red wine. Others scrubbed the town's outdoor hockey rink where a tent was set up for dance performances as well as social dancing.

Visitors to Buffalo commented that, "It wasn't just the Basque people who put this festival on. And it wasn't just for Basque people. It was the whole town." For visitors, Buffalo and Basque were briefly synonymous and this was the uniquely Basque thing about Buffalo. It was as if the changes in our lives didn't measure how Basque people were becoming less Basque, but rather how those of us who were non-Basque were becoming Basque through expressive culture.

There's one last thing I want to mention—memory. The 2011 Basque festival parade included a long line of sheep wagons, rolling one after another down Main Street. The descendants of the first herders and ranchers sat at the front of their wagons smiling and waving to the people who crowded the street. There was no advertising. No politicians running for office. Nobody hawking anything or trying to convert us to an ideology or a religion or a marketing plan. Just sheep wagons, one after another with the family names—Harriet, Auzqui, Marton, Camino, Iberlin, Inchauspe, Michelena, Esponda, and on and on. Cleaned and painted and decorated, these wagons suggested that we know we have come from somewhere to this place and that even as we stay here generation after generation we are in motion.

The sheep wagons shelter our history and house lingering spirits that live within us. Now when they have mostly been retired from ranch work, they offer us the opportunity to know who we have been and what we may now wish to be. That is what the essays in this collection originally offered—some sense of who we have been and who we might yet be.

Elisa Etchemendy of Buffalo Basque Dancers, NABO 2011, Buffalo, Wyoming.
Source: Photo by Tom Milsted, courtesy of *The Buffalo Bulletin*.

Sauveur Inchauspe sheepwagon, NABO 2011, Buffalo, Wyoming.
Source: Photo by Tom Milsted, courtesy of *The Buffalo Bulletin*.

Buffalo Zaharrer Segi Basque Dancers, NABO 2011, Buffalo, Wyoming.
Source: Photo by Tom Milsted, courtesy of *The Buffalo Bulletin*.

Jeanne Marie Etchemendy

I was born in Baigorri (St. Etienne-de-Baigorry in French), Nafarroa Beherea. I never dreamed that I would end up on a Wyoming sheep ranch. After tutoring jobs in Spain and France, I decided to visit my brothers in America. While on this trip, I met and fell in love with Pete Etchemendy, a man who was handsome, circumspect, and a gambler. One year Pete left his poker winnings in a local bartender's keep, and at the end of the year paid for our winter sheep operation.

I learned English—my fourth language—when I came to America. I've done a lot of interpreting and often assemble a new word from two languages. One such word, *Buffalotarrak*, means the one who lives in Buffalo. I have an idea that the name we Basques use for ourselves—*Euskaldunak*—may mean "the ones who stand up." Literally, *eskuak* means hands, and *dunak*, "the ones who have (hands)." This may be a reference to that distant time when the first human beings rose from walking on all fours to walking on two legs, freeing their hands.

Well, this *Euskalduna* was impressed by the great emptiness of Wyoming on that first road trip from the Casper airport to Buffalo. My memories of populated Europe included a revolution in Spain in which I hurriedly left a teaching job in 1938, and then the German occupation during the time of my next job at Angoulême, France. I like Wyoming's space and appreciate the Basque community that welcomed me to Buffalo.

---

* These introductory essays have throughout been left in the original writer's voices as they appeared in the 1996 edition (with minor editing). In some cases, such as here and with Frances Beckner Thompson, the authors have passed away, however, we believe that it is best to leave their voices as they were originally presented. —eds.

The Ones Who Stand Up

The Basque people—the *Euskaldunak*[1]—have often been called the "Mystery People of Europe," but to themselves they do not carry any aura of mystery. In Wyoming, the descendants of the emigrants from the Basque homeland have appeared to their non-Basque neighbors as hard-working, competitive, and frugal people who have, historically, kept to themselves.

Euskal Herria (in various spellings) is the *Euskaldunaks'* name for their homeland. This homeland is bounded on the west by the Bay of Biscay. It extends southeast into the plains of northern Spain and northeast into the Pyrenees Mountains. The three small provinces of the northern Basque Country are in France. The remaining four Basque provinces are in Spain. But the seven provinces, united by language and history, are neither Spanish nor French. Euskal Herria is a nation that predates France and Spain.

Throughout the centuries, many different invaders have dominated the Basque homeland, yet the *Euskaldunak* have maintained strong linguistic, cultural, and ethnic bonds. Beginning with family, clan, and village, small republics developed in which offices of community trust were filled by election—perhaps pertinent to our time is the historical Basque prohibition on priests and lawyers serving

---

1. The following will help the reader with Basque pronunciation. The five vowels, *a, e, i, o,* and *u,* are generally pronounced as in Spanish. The letter *z* is pronounced like the English *s,* while the letter *s* is similar to English *sh.* The combination *tx* is pronounced like *ch. R* is pronounced with the tip of the tongue as in Spanish. *Al* sounds like the *y* in sky, while *j* sounds like *y* in *yes.* Except when spellings reflect usage in the Buffalo community, Basque words throughout this book will be spelled using the conventions of Batua (unified Basque) Interested readers please see Alan R. King, *The Basque Language: A Practical Introduction* (Reno: University of Nevada Press, 1994).

in legislative bodies. The seven provinces were a slow outgrowth of the republics. In their political transformation, the Basques came to have simultaneous local and national allegiances and from this came the Basque slogan *Zazpiak Bat*—the "Seven Are One." The sense that many Basque people have of themselves as a nation fuels current separatist political activity in Euskal Herria.

Much of the stereotypical "mystery" of the Basque people arises from the conflicting theories about Basque origins. The January 16, 1995 issue of *Time* reported from *The History and Geography of Human Genes* that: "The most distinctive members of the European branch of the human family are the Basques of France and Spain. They show unusual patterns for several genes, including the highest rate of Rh-negative blood type. Their language is of unknown origin and cannot be placed within any standard classification. And the fact that they live in the region adjoining the famous Lascaux and Altamira caves, which contain vivid paintings from Europe's earlier hunter-gatherers leads Cavali Svorza (one of the book's authors) to a tantalizing conclusion: 'the Basques are extremely likely to be the most direct descendants of the Cro-Magnon people, among the first modern humans in Europe.'"

Descendants of Cro-Magnon people, or later immigrants to Europe, the less than 1 million contemporary Basque speakers are maintaining one of the world's oldest languages. Euskara (the Basque language) is rich in words that deal with the lives of a people at home in hills and woods: words like mountain, *mendi*; stone, *harri*; forest, *oihan*; and crag or corner, *hegi*. Most words dealing with agriculture entered Euskara with the invading Romans, indicating a Basque woodland culture that predated agriculture. Modern words have entered Euskara, first from Latin, later from French and Spanish, and recently from English and International Computerese.

The numerical system in Euskara is based on the score and ten. To say thirty, one uses the words for twenty and ten. To say forty, one uses two twenties. Basque numbering did not go beyond the hundreds so that when the concept of a thousand was needed, the Latin word *mille* was introduced as *mila*.

In addition to physical and linguistic features, the *Euskaldunak* are distinguished from other Europeans by a number of cultural patterns. The Basque household is a physical and social entity of great permanence. On the lintel above the main entrance to all Basque houses is an inscription commemorating the founding of the house and the names of the first couple inhabiting the house. The lintel name becomes, for all social purposes, the last name of anyone who lives in the house. If a man marries and moves into his wife's house, he takes her house name and leaves his behind.

This practice is linked to the Basque sense of equality and *etxeko premu*—right of the oldest. Basque houses and land, upon the deaths of their owners, have been most commonly bequeathed to the eldest child—male or female. Basque women have long had a status of greater legal independence than was the norm in Europe until quite recently. Because of this practice of leaving all property to the eldest child, younger children have often been forced to find another way of life. Many chose to become priests or nuns, many chose the seafaring life, and many emigrated.

In Euskal Herria and in their overseas emigrant communities, the *Euskaldunak* have kept alive a vigorous performance dance tradition that has drawn the attention of outsiders since the travels of Wilhelm von Humboldt through the Basque country in the spring of 1801. The dances, many of which were originally of ritual and religious significance, are today maintained as markers of ethnic identity and pride.

Throughout the West, Basque dance troupes perform dances such as *Hegi, Zazpi Jauziak* (how it is known in Buffalo, in the Basque Country it is more commonly known as *Zazpi Jauzi* — eds.), *Bolant-Dantza*, and *Axuri Beltza*. At Basque events, when the dancers finish, the audience dances a two-part dance made up of a fandango and an *arin-arin* (also called *porrusalda*—"leek soup").

Over five hundred Basques passed through the gates of Ellis Island on their way to Wyoming. Four families listed their destination as Rock Springs. The rest were coming to Buffalo. Although members of the current generation of Wyoming Basques may be business people, politicians, artists, and professionals, most of them are descendants of the sheepherders who moved to Wyoming in the early years of the twentieth century. This history continues to shape the Wyoming Basque community.

Catherine Harriet at sheep camp around 1950, near Buffalo, Wyoming.
Source: Johnson County Library, Basque Photos collection.

Joseph P. Castelli

I am a retired United States Air Force colonel and professor emeritus at East Stroudsburg University in Pennsylvania. I graduated from West Point and later received a PhD from the University of Colorado at Boulder. I'm currently an employed toymaker and a would-be golfer.

A person might wonder how I, a non-Basque, got interested in the Basque people of Buffalo. It began, as most good things do for me, with my wife Tomi. She was doing some work through the French Council in Denver and a speaker there described a small French Basque community in northern Wyoming. I was looking for a subject for a cultural geography paper at the University of Colorado. I contacted Paul Etchepare in Cheyenne. We spent some time together and I wrote the paper for which I received a B, my professor saying my insights were interesting but "shallow."

I continued my work, though, and later made several trips to Buffalo over the course of a year and a half. With each trip I became more deeply involved with the Basque community. The Basque people of Buffalo were open and helpful to me. They answered my questions on a zillion subjects. I can't possibly name all those who helped me in my research. I can only say thank you to every Basque in Buffalo and to all the non-Basques, too, who gave me insight into how they saw their Basque neighbors.

So, have a great time, enjoy yourselves, and "stay Basque."

The Basques of Buffalo, Wyoming

Buffalo comes abruptly into view as a visitor approaches it across the Wyoming table lands. Situated in the Clear Creek Valley at the base of the Big Horn Mountains, the Johnson County seat is a town of about four thousand people. Shortly after the Civil War, the Fetterman Fight and the Wagon Box Fight took place near Buffalo. Both involved Red Cloud's campaign to stop a permanent road from running along the east face of the Big Horns. In 1892, the Johnson County War was fought between open range cattle barons and more recently arrived homestead farmers and small ranchers. This event continues to be a pivotal one in Buffalo's history and in the history of the West.

Displays in Buffalo's Jim Gatchell Museum emphasize cowboys, Indians, and soldiers, all embroiled in frontier violence. The mounted photos often show much the same image of Johnson County history, although one does see pictures of sheep and outside the museum is a permanent display of a sheep wagon. While the casual visitor may carry away only a reinforcement of the cowboy stereotype, there is another dimension to Buffalo that is available to the visitor who delves slightly deeper—the Basque dimension.

Until the winter of 1994–1995, a small bar on Main Street called the 21 Club served as a second home to the local Basque community. With the usual curtained windows and advertisements for drinks, the 21 Club looked like most small-town bars. Inside, the appearance was standard for such establishments—a long bar, a pool table in the back room, card tables and chairs, leatherette booths.

But that is where the 21 Club's similarity with other small-town American bars ended, for in the 21 Club, the language was not English. One heard bits of French, some Spanish, and a language little known to most people—Basque.

Immediately to the south of the 21 Club was the entrance to the Idlewild Hotel. After climbing the stairs to the small second floor lobby, one again heard the same unusual language. While the clientele of the Idlewild was not limited to Basques, the owners and several of the residents normally spoke Basque, particularly when they wanted to be precise.

Although the 21 Club and the Idlewild are now closed, the Basque community remains a part of Buffalo life. On Sundays at noon one can tune in and listen to the Basque Hour on Buffalo's KBBS Radio. At the beginning of each program, the announcer informs listeners that, "This is the Basque program—music, news, messages and views brought to you by and for the Basque people of Buffalo." Following this introduction, Basque is spoken, with the few announcements in English addressed to the very young.

Adrien Gachiteguy, in *The Basques of the American West*, wrote that Buffalo hosts one of the "most vibrant" Basque colonies in the region. The author may have been showing his prejudice—he is a French Basque, his book focuses on French Basques, the majority of Buffalo's Basques are from the French Basque area. Nevertheless, Buffalo contains one of the more cohesive and clearly discernible Basque colonies in the American west. The intention of this article is to briefly sketch the main outlines of this colony.

The Basque community in Buffalo does not reside in a special area. There is no Basque Village within the town to be pointed out to visitors; rather, the Basques have scattered their homes throughout the town. They have not marked the present landscape with tra-ditional Basque-type houses, with a fronton (pelota wall, *piloteku* in Batua —eds.) for handball, a Basque Catholic church or even busi-nesses that one would expect to find in a Basque village in Europe. The lack of cultural artifacts, however, has not prevented Basques from maintaining their cultural identity. Basques in Buffalo form a cohesive group that plays an important part in the community.

The Basques' uniqueness is recognized by their non-Basque neighbors. When asked for their impressions of Basques, most non-Basques of Buffalo agree that:

"They are all sheepmen."

"They are good law-abiding citizens. They drink, dance, and party a lot but they stay out of trouble."

"They come to town more often than they used to."

"All of them are Catholics."

"They are good football players."

"Every fall they have a picnic somewhere up in the mountains."

"They really are hard workers. In fact, they own most of Johnson County."

This last, "they own most of Johnson County," while not quite true, is an idea based on the very pronounced growth of Basque ownership in the county throughout the twentieth century.

The first Basque to settle in Johnson County was Jean Esponda in 1902. In 1904, Jean's brother John arrived in Buffalo. Soon other Basques followed, including Harriets, Martons, Falxas, Irigarays, Caminos, Iberlins, Etchemendys, and others. Most of the Basques went to work in the already established sheep industry and by 1969 Basque sheepmen held title to over 250,000 acres of Johnson County ranch land. These ranchers actually ranched much more land than they held deed to through Bureau of Land Management leases. It may be said that the largest single factor holding the Basque Community together is ownership of land and the operation of sheep ranches on that land.

From 1902 to 1969, the history of the Buffalo Basques as ranchers can be described in terms of three major time periods: 1902–1920, 1920–1950, and 1950–1969. Examining these three periods will give a sense of the historical circumstances of Johnson County's Basque ranchers and will illuminate the persistence of Basque ethnic identity markers.

During the period of 1902 to 1920, single Basque men came to Buffalo, acquired sheep, and established families. They typically spoke Basque, lived on the ranches and, although dispersed widely throughout the sheep-raising range, remained a tightly knit social group. As recent immigrants, who were not yet citizens and so did not have the right to vote, Basques in this period were not politically active in either local or national affairs. The newly established families, consisting of both male and female European-born Basques, were governed by Old World practices. Non-Basques viewed John Esponda as a strong leader and spokesman for the Basques and, in fact, many local non-Basques thought of Esponda as the "King of the Basques." While English was required to conduct business in the American community, Basque remained the common language of the home and through the language Basque culture was passed on to the next generation. Recreation was dominated by Basque games and entertainment such as the card game *mus* and the Basque handball game known as pelota. It was in this period that a fronton was built in Buffalo against the east wall of John Esponda's barn. The Catholic Church helped maintain Basque identity and the first celebration of the Feast of the Assumption probably took place in 1918.

Perhaps most important to Basque cohesion was the fact that Basques were economically successful as a group, having readily adapted to the flourishing sheep industry of the American community. Factors contributing to the general expansion of the local economic system were high prices for lambs and wool following World War I, and the availability of land. An awareness on the part of the Basque herders of the economic opportunities in Johnson County caused them to begin to explore buying their own ranches, and the community became permanent rather than transitory.

The period from 1902 until 1920, perhaps more than any other, was characterized by a pronounced Basque cultural identity in the Buffalo area.

The years between 1920 and 1950 saw the greatest expansion in Basque land ownership. This was also the period in which the American public school system began to have a tremendous influence on the Basques. The first generation of American-born Basques was exposed to two powerful educational systems—the Basque family and the American school.

The family changed little—it remained culturally Basque and the language of the home remained Basque. In addition, close ties were kept to family members in the Basque country with many local Basques visiting the European homeland. In Baigorri, the original home of many of Buffalo's Basque people, August fifteenth, the Feast of the Assumption, was a traditional holiday. This practice was con-tinued in the new community.

Stimulating acculturation, however, the Johnson County school system was dedicated to making Americans of its pupils, including the first generation of Basques born in Buffalo. American-born Basques who entered school unable to speak English were often ridiculed by their peers. These young Basque Americans quickly became familiar with American ways and with the English language so that, when they grew up and married, the language of the home became English except in cases when the Basque-American's spouse was born in Euskadi.

In this period, recreation, too, began to lose its Basque emphasis. The fronton was used by the first settlers and their herders, but as these aged and their numbers decreased, the fronton's importance diminished. Although transitory herders from the Basque Country kept the fronton active through the early part of the period, the first generation American-born Basques played football and basketball for Buffalo High School. More and more, their other athletic outlets also became almost totally American. However, traditional Basque dances and the card game *mus* were perpetuated.

Following the death of John Esponda in 1936, John Camino was the acknowledged King of the Basques among the non-Basque community. It appears that Camino partially filled a leadership role for the new immigrants and for transitory herders.

The traits of frugality, hard work, and desire to own land allowed the Basque community to increase its land holdings during the Depression of the 1930s, and to continue and enlarge their operations during the labor shortage years of World War II.

Important in perpetuating Basque culture during the period were the many transitory herders who placed demands on the community to retain some aspects of Basque culture. Transitory herders spoke only Basque thus requiring that first-generation Basque-Americans retain or improve their own facility in the language. The herders also needed a place to live during the off-season encouraging the maintenance of a local boardinghouse and of the Idlewild as "Basque Hotels." As was mentioned earlier, the herders' interest in pelota kept that game alive. The peak in the hiring of transitory herders came in this period, and the subsequent steady decrease in their numbers was a factor in the acculturation of younger Basques into American society.

In the years between 1950 and 1969, there was a decline in two interrelated factors that had played an important part in the maintenance of the Basque community. The first decline was in the number of herders brought into the community from the Basque homeland; the second was in the availability of land in Johnson County. During the years from 1950 to 1969, all of Europe, including the Basque Country, experienced an economic boom. The need to go abroad for employment decreased. Fewer herders came to Wyoming. At the same time there was a decrease in the availability of land in Johnson County, and thus the need for additional herders diminished. During this period, some herders who had contracted for jobs in the Rocky Mountain states did not fulfill their contracts, going instead to California to work in what seemed to be better paying jobs in dairies. These changes emphasize how important the opportunity to own land was in establishing and perpetuating the Basque community in Buffalo.

As the time they had spent in the United States and in Johnson County increased, the Basques became more active politically. They sought and gained offices in the ranching associations and on local school boards. Then, beginning in the 1970s, and following their initial forays into the world of politics, members of the Basque community served as county commissioners, as members of the local hospital board, as bank directors, as state highway commissioners, and as members of the state legislature. John Marton, a Basque-American from Buffalo, served as speaker of the House in the 1995 legislative session. For the most part, Basques, as other Americans, have become active in those areas directly affecting them.

In this third period, two educational systems still governed younger Basques: the first, the home, remained strong although Basque was not the common language; the second, the school and community, became totally American. The fronton was gone although the older generation still played *mus* and participated in Basque dancing at two annual Basque community parties.

Although first-generation Basque Americans began to attend college in this period, these Basques did not break with the community as long as they remained in the sheep industry. Art Esponda, Buffalo's first Basque Fulbright Scholar, and later a wool buyer and rancher, remained very much a part of the Basque community. The celebration of the Feast of the Assumption continued to be a positive factor in the perpetuation of Basque life. Although the Basque home came to be little different from other American homes, there remained a strong Basque social unit.

Most importantly, cultural identity continued to depend upon participation in the sheep industry. Ownership of land ensured ongoing participation in wool growing. Basque sheep ranchers operated as any American sheep rancher might, still, the intense desire to own the land the sheep graze on and to be independent, plus the willingness to work hard, singled out the Basques in Buffalo during these years.

During this third period of Basque life in Buffalo and Johnson County, Basques were rapidly being integrated into the surrounding American scene. There was little opportunity for an individual to acquire the necessary land to enter the sheep business. The almost total lack of new immigrants from Europe further removed the Buffalo Basques from their Old World roots. In terms of sheer numbers and cultural distinctiveness, this period appeared to mark the zenith of Basque community development in Johnson County. If a distinctive Johnson County Basque culture is to remain alive in the future, it will be based on identity markers other than the traditional ones of Basque language use and participation in the sheep industry.

From left to right: Marie Camino with Pete and Anita, Madeline Taberna Ardanz with Joe, Mrs. Joe Guerechit with Martin, date unknown. Source: Johnson County Library, Basque Photos collection.

Kathleen Michelena Smith

I was born in 1934 and grew up in a family of twelve brothers and sisters. My father, Sebastian Michelena, ran a band of sheep on leased land for many years before buying a ranch. As a toddler I lived with my family in a dugout between Arvada and Spotted Horse, Wyoming. The dugout had dirt floors and a canvas sheet covering the opening that served as a window, yet my mother remembers that period as one of the happiest times of her life.

We often spent the summer at one of my father's sheep camps in the Big Horn Mountains. Once I was allowed to sleep out on the sheep bed ground. Looking at the night sky fascinated me until I thought about all the animals that could "get me." I pulled the covers over my head for the rest of the night. The next day my parents heard about a bear that had been roaming the area so, to my relief, I was forbidden to sleep out again.

Each fall we went to the J.C. Penney store in Buffalo where my mother purchased us a year's supply of clothing. We marched in— Joe, Seberiano, Kathleen, Jean, Betty, Martin, Santiago, Sebastian, Juaquin, Mary Louise, Pete, and Marcina. Our shopping spree was photographed and the picture printed in the Penney's circular.

I married Clifford Smith and we moved to a ranch near Spotted Horse where I helped to research and write *The Wheel of Time*, a history of the Arvada area. I also helped to restore the old 4-G community building five miles west of the Spotted Horse Store.

Clifford and I now spend winter in Arizona and summers in Sheridan. I continue to enjoy local history, arts and crafts, traveling, and genealogy.

Visiting My Family Home

My father, Sebastian Jose Michelena, was born in the Basque province of Gipuzkoa (Guipúzcoa in Spanish) a land of 1,200 square miles. This is 768,000 acres, about half the size of the original Padlock Ranch here in northern Wyoming and southern Montana. And yet, in 1978, Gipuzkoa had a population of 171,478. In summer these numbers rise even higher as the gentle climate and expanses of beachfront make the province a popular European summer resort. It's hard to imagine.

In the fall of 1982, my mother Anna, my daughter Sandra, and I flew to Madrid, Spain. We were to visit my brother Sebastian for three weeks. While we were in Spain, Sebastian took us to visit our family in the Basque homeland.

We went first to Gipuzkoa's capital, San Sebastián, called Donostia in Basque. It was here that I saw the ocean for the first time. We watched the boats in the bay and the hundreds of sun-bathers on the beach. On a nearby hilltop, a huge statue of the Virgin Mary stretched her arms out toward the ocean.

When my father was a boy, he and his family moved from Gipuzkoa to the village of Sunbilla (Sumbilla) in the province of Nafarroa. Sunbilla, population 951, was our next stop. It was green and lush there from the regular rains and from the many cold springs in the district.

My family home is on a mountainside above Sunbilla, so we parked the car in the village and walked. The trail was steep and rocky, and I grew very tired. By the time we reached the summit, I thought I couldn't go any farther. Just over the summit, though, and a short way down the hill was their house. I walked on.

Throughout the Basque country, each house has a name instead of numbers. My family home is *Casio Galchatemborda*. My grandmother and grandfather lived here many years ago. My uncle Jose Mari still lives in the house along with two of my cousins, one of whom is single.

My uncle and cousins invited us into the kitchen where they served us *kafesnes* (coffee and milk) in big cups along with cookies, wine, and anise liqueur. They also offered cherry brandy—but only to the ladies. It was an afternoon of refreshments, hugs and tears, and talk. My daughter Sandra spoke French but my uncle and cousins did not. They spoke only Basque, which we didn't speak. I counted on my brother Sebastian and on Sandra to communicate using Spanish. With all these limitations on our ability to speak to one another, I was unable to express to them what I felt there in my family home. Still, even though I could never begin to say what it meant to me to meet these beautiful people, I feel we understood each other.

The house was like many I'd seen along the way. The outside walls were stucco. There were wooden shutters on the windows though no screens. I never saw screens on the windows in Spain and yet I never saw flies in the houses either. On the ground floor beneath the dining room, there was a spotlessly clean barn and, in the barn, I counted four big hogs, many piglets, five milk cows, and one horse.

There were three lean-to cages near the entry to the house. About fifteen chickens squawked in the first lean-to while a group of dogs huddled quietly in the second. I didn't notice what, if anything, was in the third as I was so taken by the roof made of perfect flat stones.

Above the barn was the dining room, a kitchen, bathroom, and three small bedrooms. When I walked into the dining room, I was stunned by its beauty—the delicate wallpaper, the open wooden shutters framed by lace curtains. The large dining room table was covered by a brilliant white linen tablecloth and was set with china and crystal. Against one wall was a buffet and in the corner an ancient grandfather clock. This was a simple home—the table and chairs were made by family members—and yet this room was one of great dignity and beauty. Sebastian must have noticed a look of wonder on my face for he said, "In Europe, the dining room is of great importance." I found that out.

That first afternoon we left before dusk in order to find our way safely down the mountain. The next day we returned and were served a five-course meal in that beautiful dining room. When I commented on the flowers on the table, Jose Mari told me they came from the farm. Most of the food we ate came from the farm, too—vegetables from the garden and peaches from the tree by the door. Eggs from the chickens and meat from the sheep. Milk and cheese from the cows. The wine was made from grapes grown in the family vineyard. Trout and salmon came from the Bidasoa River that runs through Sunbilla. One of my cousins told me that the English had introduced fly fishing in the area and that King Edward VII often fished between the villages of Sunbilla and Santestebam. The king would walk up and down the riverbank peering at the water.

Until the late seventies at the farm, hay was cut by hand and stacked around a pole near the barn. Then one of my cousins built a hay shed and bought a small power mower that could be pushed by hand. The mower is very practical on the small steep fields and my cousin is proud of it. Though the cutting is now done with this machine, the hay is still turned by hand using long wooden rakes made from tree limbs. Because there is so much rain, haying must be done quickly. It's hard work and the family still can't make a lot of hay so it's never used for animal bedding. Instead, a fern called bracken is cut and used for bedding. Bracken is so prolific that it must be cut to keep it from encroaching on grasslands.

One Saturday night while visiting my family, we all went to the nearby village of Oyergui, population 122, for a local *festa* (party). There was a street dance with musicians playing accordions. We danced most of the night then stayed in a lovely, inexpensive, *clean* hotel. When I woke up, I found myself covered with bedbug bites. On Sunday morning we returned to Sunbilla for Mass where I was surprised to see the men seated on one side of the church and the women on the other. I was very interested in the ancient caves of the Pyrenees that are filled with images of bison, bears, and deer, of hunters and hunted. Though I was unable to visit any of the caves, I did see the Archeology Museum of Madrid's replica of the Altamira Cave that is near Santillana del Mar on the northern coast of Spain.

I do pen-and-ink drawings of animals but rather than draw on paper, I draw on the shoulder blade bones of animals, mostly cattle, but sometimes deer or antelope. I'd imagined that my technique of drawing on bones was unique but at the Archeology Museum I saw a shoulder blade bone decorated with beautifully incised figures. This object had come from a cave in the Basque Pyrenees and was estimated to have been done around 12,000 b.c.e. My Basque ancestors were far ahead of me.

My trip to the Basque homeland affected me very much. It makes me think now of the fact that, as a child, my favorite story was *Heidi*. I dreamed of visiting such an enchanted place as existed in the story. When I stood at the kitchen window of my family home near Sunbilla and looked out across the mountain, I felt I had come to that place of enchantment. A misty fog hung over the mountain, then sunlight broke through the fog. I was spellbound. The rays from the sun cast sparkling light over the land. The Basque country in the Pyrenees Mountains had fulfilled my childhood dream.

Salt Lake City Utahko' Triskalariak Basque Dancers, NABO 2011, Buffalo, Wyoming.
Source: Photo by Tom Milsted, courtesy of *The Buffalo Bulletin*.

Dancers at August 15 Basque party in the Big Horn mountains, 1925.
Source: Johnson County Library, Basque Photos collection.

Basque herders singing with John Iberlin directing at right, early 1920s, Buffalo, Wyoming. Source: Johnson County Library, Basque Photos collection.

David Romtvedt

In 1984, I was a resident writer at the Ucross Foundation east of Buffalo, Wyoming. I was invited to give a reading at the local library and my future wife Margo was in the audience. Margo grew up helping her Basque stepfather Simon Iberlin on his ranch. I, too, began to work at the ranch. Soon I was riding a beautiful ugly bay horse named Harold. And then everyone began to refer to Harold as "David's horse." By the time I came to the ranch, the sheep were gone, replaced by cattle. I guess I was becoming a cowboy.

I worked at the ranch for ten years as a windmill hand—climbing, bolting, pulling, lifting, and running pipe in and out of the ground. One of the great moments in that time was putting in the ranch's first solar pump and well. I now serve as a professor in the MFA program for writers at the University of Wyoming and play music with the band the Fireants.

Margo and I have been married for twenty-four years. We have a twenty-three-year-old daughter named Caitlin. As I became a part of the Iberlin family, I began to go to Basque dinners and dances. I had traveled in the Pyrenees so I was aware of the Basque people, though I knew nothing about them. Now I'm the accordionist for the Big Horn Basque Dancers.

A Basque who was watching me play accordion at the North American Basque Organization Convention in Reno said, "Who are you, a Norwegian in a beret?"

"I don't know," I said, and kept playing.

Basque Music and Wyoming

The Basque people (*Euskaldunak*) are generally held to be the first modern human inhabitants of Europe. Genetic, linguistic, and historical evidence indicates that they may be the direct descendants of the Cro-Magnon peoples who lived in the present Basque homeland (Euskal Herria or Euskadi). It is ironic, then, that relatively little is known about the origins and early history of the Basque people. This is especially true of Basque language (Euskara) and arts.

The first historians to encounter the Basques were Romans, but these left few records concerning the people of the Pyrenees. The earliest known written example of Euskara dates from 980 c.e. The first Basque vocabulary appeared in a twelfth-century codex, but included only eighteen Basque words. The first work printed in Euskara was a 1545 collection of religious and lyrical poems. Euskara has been maintained primarily through oral transmission.

The case is much the same for traditional Basque music. Only in the nineteenth and twentieth centuries have written collections of Basque music been made. It's clear that early music had spiritual power and marked major occasions in the lives of individuals and communities. But that tells us very little about either music sound or meaning.

There are three ancient Basque musical instruments that give some sense of musical continuity in Euskadi. The first is the *txistu*, a three holed end-blown pipe that is held and fingered by the left hand while the right hand simultaneously keeps time on a small drum that is suspended from the bent elbow of the left arm. The second instrument is the *alboka*, a double-tubed cane pipe. The *alboka*'s tubes are joined along their length and each tube has a reed on one end. The reeds are enclosed in a cow horn that serves as the mouthpiece of the instrument. *Alboka* players use circular breathing to produce a continuous sound somewhat like that of the bagpipe. The third instrument is the *dultzaina*, a double reed wind instrument with an intense penetrating sound. Two *dultzainas* are usually played together accompanied by a third musician playing a drum.

While the *txistu*, *alboka*, and *dultzaina* are among the oldest Basque musical instruments, the instruments most associated with traditional Basque music and dance today—both in the Basque homeland and in emigrant communities—are the diatonic button accordion and the more recently developed piano accordion.

The button accordion was invented in 1825 and was probably in use in Euskadi by the mid to late nineteenth century. Although its introduction met with opposition—those who disliked the accordion called it *infernuko auspoa* (the Devil's bellows)—it very quickly became the center of community music. It was loud, sturdy, and capable of playing rapid complex melodies. It could also accompany itself with both chords and rhythm.

One of the forms of music that developed following the introduction of the button accordion was *trikitixa*. The word is onomatopoetic for the push-pull breathing sound of the button accordion and came to mean both the instrument itself and the style of duet music made by a button accordion and a *pandero* (tambourine). In *trikitixa* music the *pandero* is played with the fingertips so as to produce a glittering continuous percussive drive that mirrors the rapid melodic passages played on the accordion. *Trikitixa* is widely played today.

In whatever form, and from whatever province in Euskadi, Basque immigrant communities around the world have kept alive a performance tradition in which music and dance are inseparable. The experience of the Basques of Buffalo, Wyoming, is in many ways parallel to that of other small Basque towns in the American west.

In Buffalo, as in other towns, the Basque community has formed a club that has been the sponsor of the local dance troupe—the Big Horn Basque Dancers. The troupe is made up of children and young people from Basque families. For a few of the dances, the accompaniment is provided by the *txistu* but most dances are performed to the music of a single accordion.

The Big Horn Basque dance group was formed at a time when people feared the loss of an identifiable Basque community. The purpose of the dance group is community maintenance. In using music and dance as markers of ethnic pride and identity, the Buffalo dancers and those from other American Basque communities give great attention to replicating dances as they would be performed in Euskadi. Dance troupe directors travel to Europe to see the dances performed there. In the United States, these directors consult older dancers as to the traditional forms of the dances. The directors also communicate with one another as to the "correct" performance of particular dances. Videotapes of prominent European and American dance troupes (such as the Oinkari dancers of Idaho) are traded around. If no other troupe is performing a particular dance, it may even be reconstructed from oral or written descriptions.

Throughout the American West, Basque dance troupes—including Buffalo's—perform many of the same songs and dances—*Hegi*, *Zazpi Jauziak* (*Jauzi* in Batua though in Buffalo people say jauziak for this dance name), *Bolant-Dantza*, *Axuri Beltza*, *Banako*, *Diana Donostia*, *Makil Haundia*, *Baztan Dantza*, and others. Dance troupes try to include dances from many, if not all, of the seven Basque provinces. The dances must identify the local Basque community without excluding regions of the original Basque homeland that may not be represented in the American group.

In the past, performances have taken place at Basque-only community events—at dinners or picnics, in celebration of Catholic holidays (especially the August fifteenth Feast of the Assumption of Mary), or as part of large family gatherings. In recent times there has been an increasing sense that the dances can and should be performed at non-Basque public events. In Buffalo, it has been suggested by both Basque and non-Basque members of the business community that the dances should be performed as part of a consciously organized campaign to increase tourism, to help the town to profit from the presence of its "colorful" Basque citizens.

Basque dance can be divided into two parts—performance dancing and social dancing. The local troupe, after formal rehearsal sessions, will present dances to the community. After this performance, audience members will be invited to dance one or more widely known dances from the performance repertoire with the troupe. The last of these dances will be a fandango—the most popular social dance among the Basque people both in Buffalo and throughout the West. The fandango acts as a bridge between the performance dances and the social dances—polkas, waltzes, schottisches—that follow the performance.

The fandango is done in two parts. The first part is in 3/4 time but played so rapidly that it becomes 6/8 in feel. The second part, the *arin-arin*, is in 2/4 time and always follows the 3/4 section to end the dance.

Both the performance dances and the social fandango are intricate and precise. Both mean more to Basque people than motion, color and sound. In Euskadi, in the American west, and in Buffalo, music and dance are important markers of ethnic identity.

The importance of these art forms in the continuance of a distinct people is partly seen in the fact that Basque folkloric dance performances were outlawed for the first twenty-five years of the Franco government in Spain. Such dances were perceived by Franco as inflammatory of nationalist or separatist sentiments.

Related to the prohibition on the dances in Spain, some American Basques have presented their dance troupes in purely aesthetic terms. There is a sort of cultural schizophrenia in this since the dance troupes have usually been formed in order to emphasize Basque identity. Still, the attempt to make the dances non-threatening to the broader community is understandable in light of Basque history in the United States.

The first Basques in the American West were often despised by native-born Americans. The Basques were itinerant herders who entered the West at the end of the days of the open range. They were interlopers and their strange unknown language marked them as more foreign than foreign. Basques had to prove themselves "good Americans."

In the course of this century the image of the Basques has changed dramatically. They have gone from despised newcomer to romantic hero and hard worker. Outsiders frequent Basque restaurants and Basque festivals. These outsiders take away a new image of the hearty Basques who live for good food and wine, for sport and dance. As William A. Douglass has stated, "American society is most tolerant of ethnic differences in the areas of cuisine and innocuous folk arts."

Aware of this and aware too of how recently they were reviled, some Basques have sought to present their dance as one such "innocuous folk art." One American dance troupe director has said that when he returned from studying music and dance in Euskadi, some members of his community were reluctant to send their children to participate in his performance group. They feared that the director's commitment to the preservation of the regional dances was a mask for ETA sympathies. (ETA—*Euskadi ta Askatasuna* "Basque Land and Liberty"—the violent militant wing of the Basque separatist movement, which, at the time of publication of the new edition in November 2011, has just announced a permanent end to its nearly thirty years of armed activity, a historic announcement. —eds.)

The Buffalo, Big Horn Basque Dancers's repertoire has an especially evocative dance—*Zazpi Jauziak*. This dance is one of the first taught to children and normally only children perform the dance.

Basque dance is shaped by the history of the Basque people, by their centuries of struggle for independence, by their experience in isolated rural communities of the American West. In this social and historical context, the dance is more than just "art."

Zazpi Jauziak means "seven jumps" and refers to the fact that there are seven Basque provinces. While each is separate from the others with differences in dialect, history, and customs, the seven make up one Basque nation.

The music and dance for *Zazpi Jauziak* are in three sections. The first and second sections each include a few of the basic steps that go into making many Basque dances. The third section is simply one bar of music.

After the first playing of sections one and two, the young dancers leap as high as they can into the air while audience members shout out *"bano!"* After the second playing of sections one and two, the one-bar-long third part is played twice. The dancers leap twice and the audience members shout out with the leaps, *"bano! biga!"* This goes on seven times so that the last time through, the one-bar third part is played seven times, the dancers leap seven times and the audience members call out, *"bano! biga! hiru! lau! bost! sei! zazpi!"*[1] This marks the dance as complete.

Zazpi jauziak offers both musical and social completeness. Musically, there is the relaxed feel of parts one and two played again and again, followed by the tension of the increasing number of leaps. Socially, community members are aware of the historical meaning of the dance, of the presence, if only symbolically, of Basque unity, and of the hope of maintaining Basque identity into the future. Young dancers and older audience members are brought together and both share in a history that, through dance, remains alive.

---

1. This is essentially counting to seven, although the numbers for one and two are variations to Batua numbers *bat* and *bi* —eds.

1920: Buffalo: Amatxi, Grandmother, the Dignity of Work for Jeanne Etchemendy Iberlin

No topsoil, no shuffle and leap to the shouts of the fandango. No Saturday Jai-alai. No Sunday walks in the sweet sun, the music playing from the leaves on the trees. No rain, no rolling down deep, green, soft hillsides. No home, no friends, no family.

Sometimes for this woman, this human being who for fifty years will be known to all as Amatxi, it seems there is only nothing, plenty of nothing. But it's not true. As sure as the snow will fall again and bathe this empty land in brilliance and beauty, there is something. There is the dignity of work. She meditates on this and smiles secretly for herself. The man who thinks the worker doesn't meditate on the meaning of her acts is a fool or an owner.

A single woman among forty lonely sheepherders, she was married within months of arriving here. He was a shy man, quiet though not really dignified. How he caught this belle of the west is a mystery about which no one has a clue.

She walks twice a day from her house in town to a pasture a mile away. Twice a day she milks her cow. Letting her hands rise from her pockets, she warms them under her arms, blows across her fingertips. Gently, she squeezes and pulls, sliding the inside of her thumb and palm along the cow's pink, shining skin. She turns the cow's udder so the snow-white milk strikes the pail obliquely, the way rain strikes a windowpane and slides without splashing. The bucket full, she hefts it up and walks home. She follows the same route each day and each day sees how this town is more like the Basque homeland, more like the world than she would have thought, how all three are ever-changing and ever the same.

Work gives a woman a sense of place, she thinks. "And it gets me tired," she laughs out loud, making over her husband's worn, wool shirts for her son Simon, sitting up for him when he is out late at night.

How little she needs to sleep, the woman awakened by her chores, by her task, by life. And some days it seems she will live forever. The work is always waiting. The chickens in the yard, the pig in its pen. Now it's time to kill the pig, make cured pork, make lard, make sausages, make ham. Now it's time to can vegetables—the beans, carrots, cabbages, tomatoes, all the wealth of the reluctant earth.

Not to mention sheep—moving sheep, doctoring sheep, shearing sheep, docking sheep, branding sheep. Five thousand sheep, and on the day when the bank takes the three thousand best youngest animals to pay the mortgage, it's almost a relief. Two thousand old ewes to begin again. Either way it's a sea of work, the only sea lapping at life here on the plains. It is truly crazy, but it's worth it—life.

"Hard, shmard," she says, trying out American slang, "What did you expect from any place on this earth? The wind blows one way then the next. Some days the wind blows from every direction at once. Some days there's no wind at all. It's a hundred degrees. I can dream of the rustling leaves, or I can reach up and shake the branch."

She reaches up and makes the leaves rustle, and a bird sings, lifting and gliding in the air above Buffalo, Wyoming.

1989: Buffalo: Aitatxi, Grandfather, a Weed

Sitting at the Buffalo Bar, nursing beer after beer then getting up to leave. And it's a long haul back to somewhere else. Just north of town, a pickup pulls onto the shoulder, and the driver gets out to take a leak. That's not so uncommon what with the distance between buildings and toilets here, and with the many ways a man's bladder can become pinched and full.

For the driver, there's no relief, and he stops again two miles up the road at the Rock Creek exit, parks the pickup right there in the lane, this time under the roof of the interstate. There's no place to pull off, and another pickup is coming down the road.

Sam Jensen is on his way home. He sees the pickup stopped on the road and notices a man between it and the retaining wall. The man is squatting as if he had been suddenly struck by the need to defecate. "Poor guy," Jensen thought, and drove wide around him, looking away to allow the man a little privacy.

When Jensen comes back the man is gone, the pickup is gone, the road covered with blood. What kind of an animal could have left that much blood on the road?

The night black clouds spin by over the red blood of Lucien Laurent Millox, who cannot see. Over his face the interstate makes a wall through which he cannot ascend, and the pickups churn by, one after another driven by men he does not know. Lucien is dead, and even if he were only almost dead, and able to groan and turn and the interstate were to disappear, there would still be the fact of his face being smashed, his bloody, blackened eyes swollen shut.

Born in Baiona, France, Lucien attended school in a convent. During World War II, there were the eternal Pyrenees Mountains, reminding one that all things will pass, that only change will remain. After the war, there was the foreign legion and then the United States, Johnson County, Wyoming, where Lucien, a stoutly built man was known as a good worker.

Yesterday at age sixty-three, Lucien stood firmly at the border dividing good worker from old age.

Lucien Laurent Millox is dead. Someone beat him with a blunt tool, a hammer maybe, a steel pipe, the flat of a shovel. Under the night sky filled with stars, the night sky that is a bowl and the stars needles of light that hurt your eyes when you look. And the stars are eyes, too, that look down on Lucien's nakedness.

It is no shame to be stripped of all that we have. Before birth, after birth, it isn't hard to be who you are.

Lucien Laurent Millox, Basque sheepherder, is dead. They pick up his body and carry it to the church, and the priest tells the brief story of Lucien's life, how he worked on farms in the Basque homeland and on ranches in the Big Horn Mountains.

"He was as important as Gorbachev," the priest says. And more to the point, "He was as important as the Pope." That makes everyone think.

Sometimes Lucien drank too much then he'd offer to fight with you, or he'd pull out a wad of bills and suggest you pool your money with him and buy a ranch. He was as important as the Pope. Each of us is as important as the Pope, including the man who murdered Lucien.

After Mass, the battered body is carried away for burial. Domingo Martirena, Mike Iriberry, Charles Marton, Arturo Vasco, John Esponda, and Mitch Esponda lift Lucien to their shoulders and begin to walk. The heavy box is a little unbalanced but the six are able to carry Lucien away and home.

We have all hefted thousands of coffins and know that each one carries a brother or sister. The pallbearers are brothers. And the murderer is not simply despised, but is a despised brother.

After the funeral, three-year-old Matthew Iberlin Spotted Calf, half-Basque, half-Rosebud Lakota returns to his home and struggles to help his uncle busy himself pulling dandelions from the lawn.

"Why do you pull flowers?" Matthew asks.

"I don't want them here in the lawn," his uncle says, "They're weeds that will take over the lawn; they'll spread and soon there'll be no grass."

The uncle pulls the dandelions with a long steel tool. Matthew asks to help and is handed the tool. The boy shoves the steel into the ground and works to pull up the plant. Mostly he only gets the blossom, and the root remains deep in the earth. After two or three attempts, he speaks again, "How do you say *weed* in Basque?"

But this is Wyoming, not Baiona. So many possible words—how to say *weed* in English, how to say *weed* in Lakota how to say *weed* in Basque. Would the squatting murderer know the word weed in any language? Would it be our word for the same plant?

The uncle says, "I don't know how to say *weed* in Basque, Mateo. You'll have to go and ask your Grandfather Aitatxi. He'll know the word."

With Simon at Four Mile Ranch

Because Four Mile is fairly large and because the windmills are spread over the entire ranch, we spend a lot of time driving to work. We have to take the rig truck in order to pull the pipe from the ground, or to lift the fan and head off. We take the Ford pickup with the flatbed box, too—it has the hand tools. Sometimes when a tower has begun to slip into the ground and so must be straightened we need the backhoe. We use the winch on the gold Jeep to haul the tower back up to plumb and hold it in place while we repair the corner posts. I have many times imagined the taut cable snapping and whipping through the air, slicing me in half.

After the tower is plumb, we dig a five-foot-deep hole around each corner and cement the tower in place—hand mixing and shoveling the cement into the hole. We haul in bags and bags of ready-mix. The Ford's flatbed is perfect for this.

Sometimes as we're working on a mill, we discover a problem we hadn't foreseen and we have to drive back to the buildings for a part, or to jimmy doodle a temporary part until we can find the right thing.

The roads are dirt tracks, often little more than two faint shadows six or eight feet apart. Some of the roads are sand, some clay. In a few places, large jagged rocks fill the right-of-way. In spring, when it rains, the gumbo clay turns into a slick sheet—"slick as snot," they say. Then the way is nearly impassable. The wheels spin, the truck wallows sideways. Great globs of clay are thrown up by the tires. The clay spatters the fenders, doors, windshield. It covers the mirrors. If the windows are open, it flies inside, splattering our clothing and faces. In summer the dust rises and is sucked into the cab of the truck nearly choking us.

The roads are best in winter when the earth is frozen and covered with hard-packed snow. But those conditions are rare. More often the wind has scoured the earth bare in one place while nearby there is a drift of snow rising like a wall before us. Simon usually tries to blast through the drifted snow. Usually we make it. Now and again we don't. In which case, we dig the truck out or we walk to get another truck to winch the stuck one out.

When we are riding together, Simon tells me the story of the ranch. I was going to say the history of the ranch, but story is more accurate. For the telling is part fact, part dream, part longing, part resignation, part love, and part resentment. The story is rich, full, and present. In Simon's story there is no past, only the perpetual present of Four Mile and those who have worked it.

After several years during which we have worked together on the two windmills in the Morrison Pasture, Simon tells me the pasture's story. The man who homesteaded this spot, and for whom the pasture is named, was Mr. Morris.

"If his name was Morris, why is this the Morrison Pasture?

"We just call it Morrison cause it's easier to say. We've always called it that."

There's a rough board cabin as we enter the pasture.

"Old Man Morris's place. For as long as I knew, he lived there alone, eating nothing but oatmeal and drinking nothing but coffee." Simon points up behind the cabin about a hundred yards where there's a slight oval depression and a few rotten fenceposts.

"That was the reservoir. He had it fenced so that the sheep couldn't get in. It was the drinking water for him and his horses. He didn't want sheep walking around in it, turning it into a mud bog. Old Man Morris lived in this cabin year round. He never bathed— put his winter clothes on in the fall and wore them until spring.

"During World War II, when Morris was about seventy-five years old, the sheriff asked my dad to look after the old man. When I'd come into town, I'd stop there to check on him. We had an old

Ford pickup. This was before four-wheel drive, that didn't come till after the war, you know. One day I came slipping and sliding down here toward Morris's cabin. I spent the last half mile or so working on getting the truck stopped.

"I banged on the door but Old Man Morris didn't answer. I could see him through the one small window in the cabin. The window glass was always sooty and gray so Old Man Morris looked like a dirty, fire damaged ghost. He was puttering around the stove, fussing with a few little sticks of cottonwood. I pounded harder on the door, then I shouted his name. I kept at it like that, pounding and shouting for a half an hour but he never heard me. He'd latched the door from the inside so I couldn't open it and stick my head in. Always latched the door, not to keep anyone out but to keep the wind from ripping the door open and off its hinges. I was about to give up and go when he opened the door to throw out a pail of dirty water. 'Hai, Simon, what are you doing there standing in the cold? You waiting for spring?' Then he laughed at me.

"He had an ear infection and couldn't hear so it didn't exactly matter what I answered. I motioned to him to ask how he was. He said fine. I asked him to come to town with me and have his ears checked but he refused. I kept asking and he kept refusing. When I turned to leave, he said, 'You better be careful, standing around the door to people's cabins, you're gonna get hit with a bucket of dirty water and froze to death.' I went on into Buffalo but told my dad and the sheriff who came out and took Morris to the doctor who said the old man should stay in town for the winter. There was an ex-whore-house that'd been made into a boarding house for elderly bachelors. 'Too bad.' is what Morris said.

"During that winter he spent in town, someone broke into his cabin and stole his saddle, tack, tools. Cleaned him out. That was 1943."

When we come to Four Mile, it's usually by driving out the interstate to Schoonover Road and then southeast on the county road to Harriet's and onto the ranch. Sometimes we come through Morrison's. We get off the interstate at Dry Creek, turn onto Esponda's and drive toward Ruby's. At Ruby's, we cross Crazy Woman Creek and climb a steep ridge onto a sloping bench. We go southeast, through land covered by sage and several grasses. In spots there are bitter-brush and greasewood. Only in the watercourses are there trees—cottonwood. I'm always struck by how spare the land is and yet how varied it is. This is the landscape of almost all the Basque ranches in the county.

Driving this way, the Big Horns shimmer behind our right shoulders. In May the mountains remain covered by snow and it's not uncommon for us to get new snow during May even at the base of the mountains.

During the spring storm of 1984, it snowed continuously for the first five days of May. In town the drifts were fifteen feet high. The porch of our house was completely filled by snow. Margo opened the back door and began to dig the snow away, bringing it into the house and putting it in the bathtub where it melted and was later used to water houseplants.

After she'd carved out a small opening in the wall of snow, she began to shove lumps of snow forward. When the hole was large enough, she crawled out onto the porch just below the roof, strapped on her skis and, hunched over like a racer, sped down the slope into the backyard and across the buried lawn to her shop. There were dead songbirds everywhere. They had already returned north and in a frenzied attempt to escape the storm had bashed themselves against the windows. Now they lay silently on the glittering snow. In death their color had left them. Even the crimson blood on their feathers had frozen to a dull brown. As the snow melted, more dead birds appeared. Throughout that summer Margo found the occasional body among the underbrush in the flower beds.

After that storm, half the sheep in the county were dead and, for several years, there were no deer at Four Mile and only a few prong-horn. This year in early May, I saw ten pronghorn in the Morrison Pasture, and fourteen mule deer. Near the gas plant well, there was a huge flock of tiny birds peeping and running furiously about. I heard the meadowlarks calling off and on all day. A red-tailed hawk hung above the West Bridge mill.

The Bridge Pasture has its own little story. For years, it was impossible to ford Four Mile Creek along a several mile stretch so Simon built a bridge. As soon as that bridge was finished, the creek stopped running and hasn't run since. The bridge long ago rotted and has disappeared. We drive the trucks down the steep incline into the creek bed and then grind back out in four wheel drive low. All that's left of the creek's water is the name Bridge Pasture.

The U.S. geological survey maps call the Hay Draw, "Whiskey Draw," a name that's left from Prohibition. Now there's neither water nor whiskey, neither hay nor grain.

Four Mile is filled with little liquid problems and enticements. There are three fuel tanks behind the work shed near the corrals. Each of these is operated with a hand pump. You pump the lever slowly and evenly up and down and the gasoline or diesel is forced out. But no matter how smoothly and evenly you pump, the gas comes out in a gushing spurt followed by a pause. The process is so slow that if you leave the engine running on some of the large machines they will burn fuel faster than you can put it in the tank. Four Mile's is a short history of liquid.

The Hupp Draw is named for Mr. Hupp. The draw is seven miles from the Four Mile cabin. To get there you rise with the land to the east, half circle through a series of ridges, cross an expanse of boulders and sandstone and, finally, come down a steep narrow eroding hill into the draw, hidden at the bottom of a hole. It's hard to get in there now and would have been very hard indeed sixty years ago.

This is the spot where Mr. Hupp set up equipment to distill whiskey. It's far from the Whiskey Draw, but it's only a short distance to the water in Powder River and it's atop a coal bed Hupp used to make fire. When he finished the whiskey, he hauled it to town and sold it.

Then there's poison. I think of the ranchers walking up and down their draws or riding on four wheelers, spraying for cockleburs. Spraying and spraying and the sickly sweet but sharp smell of the herbicide drifts through the dry air.

As we leave Ruby's place behind, we keep moving southeast along the ridge. There's a draw to our west and on the next ridge past it, there are a few scattered remnants of buildings.

"After World War I," Simon says, "there was a lot of homesteading in Powder River country. People thought they'd come out here and get their own place, be farmers. To the Midwesterners the 640 acres they could get under the arid lands amendment to the Homestead Act sounded like a lot. They had no idea you couldn't make it with 640 acres. They tried dry farming and a lot of them, hardy souls, scrabbled by during the twenties, but there were five or six years of bad drought in the thirties. Lot of people talk about how ranchers now have to have jobs in town to support their ranching habit. It was the same then. The men worked the oilfields down at Midwest, south of Kaycee. They'd be gone all week, the women doing the work on the homestead. There was a one-room school on that ridge, had about ten students in the early thirties. By World War II almost everyone had left to work in the shipyards on the coast. The school was abandoned, but the building sat there on the ridge for years. I don't remember when it was torn down."

I look across the draw and think about that little community complete with its own school. Now it's just another ridge on Four Mile. Sixty years ago there were people all over this land. Simon points out a piece of ground under a cutbank. "Four Basque bachelors each had a homestead there. You can see the corner where the four pieces met. Under the homestead law a person had to show that he was living on his land and that he was making improvements— buildings, fences. He had to do this in order to get clear title to the land after five years. These four Basques built one cabin that sat on the four corner boundary. They lived together in the cabin and each one claimed it as an improvement on his homestead."

There are homestead remains all over Four Mile. In the Bridge Pasture there's a deep cistern near the water course. It's rocked in to slow seepage of water into the earth. We've covered the top to keep animals and people from tumbling in. Out near the West Bridge mill there's a dugout. The earth has collapsed on it, forming what looks like a miniature volcano. When I get down on my hands and knees and peer into the foot high hole in the side of the earth, I can see that this is indeed human work.

There are twisted cracked support beams and a litter of wood and metal on the earth. Simon counsels against going in as the whole thing may collapse. "Someday I want to get the backhoe in here and open this up," he says, "see what's inside."

Out near the south boundary of the ranch is another dugout. And way out in the roughest barest land—the breaks going toward Powder River—there's a spot on a ridge that's high and lonesome, commanding an open view of the Big Horns to the west and the jagged breaks to the east. Here, a homesteader ambitiously built a cabin and brought his Midwestern wife to live. His wife brought her household furnishings and was aghast when she saw her new home. The cabin was several miles from the river so there was no water, no power, and no road.

"That guy's wife wasn't very happy here." Simon says. "Finally, in a big wind, the cabin blew over and crumpled in a heap as it tipped over the edge of the ridge."

What's left is a smooth patch of black earth, sparkling where there are bits of mica and granite, along with crushed china and crystal goblets.

Just before the Four Mile boundary, coming in from Schoonover, there's a flat. Two bachelor brothers, Clyde and Ike Rickett, homesteaded here, and built their one-room cabin. Clyde planted corn on the flat and for years he successfully raised his crop. He had no water for irrigation and there was no more rain on his corn field than anywhere else in Powder River country. He planted in rows four feet apart, each plant several feet from the next, then cultivated the field several times each season and mulched around the plants. He fenced the field. Outside the fence the grass was burning up in the dry heat, but inside, his corn was deep green. You could hear the leaves rustling in the hot wind. The cool life of the leaves pushed itself up and away, making a tiny convection current over the cornfield, a drift of air that was almost refreshing.

Clyde had a two-horse team with which he pulled a large heavy wheel that turned the earth between his wide corn rows. He spoke with a stutter and as he walked behind his horses he called to them, "Hey, there, M-M-M-M-Maud, m-m-m-m-move along there, M-M-M-M-Maud."

"You could hear Clyde calling to Maud from up here at the Four Mile corrals, a mile from him and his brother Ike's fields." Simon pauses.

In *The Unknown Craftsman*, Soetsu Yanagi says, "Every artist knows that he is engaged in an encounter with infinity." Yanagi says that's what art is. It's what ranching is, too. Someone ought to write a book called *The Unknown Rancher*.

Simon speaks again. "Each brother had his own field. Clyde's always did better. No matter how dry it was he somehow managed to get a crop of corn out of this soil."

I look at the open flat and try to imagine corn growing there. It's very nearly impossible to imagine it much less to have done it.

"Even though he knew how to survive here, Clyde left right after World War II. That's almost fifty years ago, but you know, sometimes, I'll be up at the corrals working and I can hear Clyde calling out, 'Hey, M-M-M-M-Maud.'"

Simon turns and looks down on the airstrip flat below the fields. I've been with him enough to know that Dick Green homesteaded that spot. Dick had a suitcase of photographic negatives showing his homestead life. He'd taken pictures of everything—the building of his cabin, breaking the earth, planting and nurturing crops, his tools and machines, the cottonwoods along the water course, the hills. When Dick's cabin burned down, all those photographs, including the negatives, were lost.

In *This House of Sky*, Ivan Doig wrote: "Simply, it came down to this: homesteads of 160 acres, or even several times that size, made no sense in that vast and dry and belligerent landscape of the high mountain west. As well try to grow an orchard in a window box as to build a working ranch from such a patch."

So what if, I say to myself, you've got a landscape and weather as difficult as any Doig knew, and people who not only don't have enough land to ranch, but are trying to farm! To farm where the precipitation may be sixteen inches a year, or twelve, or eight or six. Where the last frost will be in late May or early June. Where the first frost will be sometime in August, or maybe September if you're lucky. Where the summer highs will be over a hundred degrees and the wind will blow hot and dry, sucking the water out of everything. Where the winter lows will be twenty, thirty, or forty below, reaching fifty-four below one night two winters ago.

Well, Mr. Clyde Rickett was farming. He knew something about corn but he must also have known something about infinity and vision. I'd like to see Clyde walking around here inspecting each corn plant, then looking up into the sky. Water and sky—the religion of life as it is.

Simon explains to me the importance of keeping sheep out of the new fresh succulent delicious sweet clover in spring. He says, "There's nothing those sheep would like better than to eat that clover. But sweet clover is an anticoagulant. The sheep eat it, then you dock and when the knife takes that lamb's tail off, the blood gushes out. It's hard on most lambs, kills some of them. A lamb's not normally going to bleed to death from docking. But if they've been eating clover . . ."

We walk over to put a charger on the battery of the dump truck and see that the cows have broken down the fence to get to the hay. They broke through the fence in two spots and then managed to pull almost the entire thing down, trampling it and jerking barbed wire all over. We'll put in new fence posts and string new wire, and then we'll have a corral. But it'll be empty of feed, enclosing not hay but dust and manure.

We saw two pairs of mallards, one at the Hupp Draw mill then later in the day one at the South Pasture West mill. I think they were the same pair. They had flown ahead of us from Hupp to the South Pasture. At the South Pasture electric mill there were several killdeer and, nearby, a sage hen. Skittering near the ground in front of the truck were hundreds of lark buntings, flying like a loosely defined single creature.

Until World War II, work at Four Mile was done with horse teams. "We always had four, five, or six work horses—big horses, 1,800 or 1,900 pounds. We always had a few saddle horses, too. Didn't need them much, what with running a sheep operation."

In Edward Abbey's *The Brave Cowboy*, the hero, coming to visit a friend he's not seen in a long time, is asked what he's been doing. He answers, "I was afraid you'd ask me that . . . I can't lie to you, neither; sure wish I could, it's so downright shameful."

The cowboy's friend guessed. "Don't tell me you've been herding sheep again!"

And he, "Jerry, you're absolutely right. Yessir, I've been playing nursemaid to God's lowliest critters. So help me . . ."

The conversation went on about like this, with the friend saying, "At this rate you'll end up on a dude ranch, Jack."

And Jack responding, "You're right; when a man's fallen to herding sheep he might as well go all the way down."

Then Simon tells me, "All day we'd melt snow in a rendering kettle to make water for the horses to drink. Now a horse out on winter range can get plenty of water from eating snow, but if that horse is working he needs more water than he can get from snow alone. I'd spend hours chopping sage for fire and filling a big cooking pot with snow. Takes a lot of snow to make a little water."

Those horses were hauling a sled, taking feed to sheep. Again and again Simon tells me the merits of sheep and the faults of cows. "Oh, there isn't an animal on this earth dumber than a cow, except maybe the man who owns one. In winter, a cow won't eat snow—you've got to water that cow all winter long. Sheep'll get all the water they need from snow. And in spring they'll get water from dew. Think a cow would try that? No, sir."

Simon and I have spent a lot of time repairing stock tanks. The traditional tank is a steel trough, either rectangular or circular, which sits on the ground. It's designed so that a cow can walk up to the tank, put its face in the water, and drink. But that isn't what a cow does. If it can, a cow will walk right into the tank. And all cows bash the sides of the tanks, bend and break the bottoms. The usual defense is to build a fence around the tank which will allow the cow to get its head into the water but not its body into the tank. Then the cows shove on the fence until they break it and can wreck the tank.

Simon and I were out replacing a metal stock tank. It was before Simon had gotten the idea to use the giant tires from coal trucks. When we lifted the frail steel floor, we exposed a family of mice that skittered madly away. I could almost see the eagles and owls pouncing on them.

As a top-of-the-food-chain predator, I wonder a great deal about other predators and about the predator's role in the health of the biological web. The cruelty of it bothers me, and I don't understand it very well though I defend predators when ranchers say we need to get rid of them.

A fox or coyote may kill a lamb then bite through the lamb's side to eat the curdled milk in the stomach. Mountain lions have been known to kill a lactating ewe and eat only the udder. Both bobcats and lions, after killing an animal, will drag the viscera away so as not to contaminate the meat. A coyote will often grab a lamb by the neck. This may constrict the lamb's neck so that the animal suffocates or it may break the lamb's neck. All of these predators will occasionally kill an animal and eat only the liver, kidneys, lungs, or other delicacy. An eagle can pick up a lamb and fly away with it. What can the lamb be thinking as it disappears into the heavens?

Four Mile has a large prairie dog population. The prairie dog's natural predator is the black-footed ferret. The ferret is nearly extinct. It was, in fact, believed to be extinct until a small group was discovered near Meeteetse, Wyoming in the early 1980s. Wyoming Game and Fish has been nurturing this ferret population in the hope of releasing substantial numbers back into the wild.

In the meantime, the prairie dog's most ardent predator is man. I say man meaning not human beings, but men—fat, thin, young, old, drunk, sober. Men seem to love shooting prairie dogs for pleasure.

One day, leaving the ranch exhausted after working on a wind-mill we never got to pump right, we came upon two men and two teenaged boys leaning over the hood of a pickup. They cradled their rifles in their arms, firing fairly often, talking and laughing. Simon pulled up and rolled down the pickup window.

Nods all around. Silence, then, "How you doing?"

"We're target shooting prairie dogs." One of the men said, and one of the young boys explained, "Yeah, if you hit 'em right, they just explode before your eyes, like a watermelon." His eyes lit up and he described how the pieces of prairie dog fly off in every direction. "Got to hit 'em right, though."

We went home. Simon said, "Not worth making a stink about."

Soetsu Yanagi said, "Seeing comes first. See first and know afterwards."

The difference between knowing the names of things and know-ing the country. Knowing both how to take care of the earth and how to care for the earth. How is it that the fox biting through the lamb's stomach knows without knowing while the men and boys blowing up prairie dogs don't know while knowing?

I don't ask Simon that question. Everything I have observed of him in ten years tells me that he is thinking about it and that, as yet, neither of us has the answer.

There's one last story. Each year in June, the sheep were moved from winter pasture at Four Mile up to summer pasture in the Big Horns. The move took several days. Ranchers and herders walked slowly with the sheep, struggling to keep them together, to get them where they needed to be each night without frightening the spooky animals, without losing any of them.

"I was moving the sheep and my dad was going to come that night with food and water. I had a little bit of bread inside my shirt but it wasn't even really lunch just a snack. I was hungry. In the late afternoon, it began to rain hard. I was soaked, cold, hungry, tired. My dad never showed up. I got the sheep bedded down but couldn't sleep myself. I ate the bread. I was miserable. The next morning my dad finally showed up and we had a huge breakfast and I got dry clothes then it was time to move the sheep again. Ha! That's it."

That's it. At Four Mile, the ghosts are not ghosts, they are presences, passing with us over the land. Then we are both on our way.

Simon and Dollie Iberlin with grandchildren Matthew and Caitlin at Buffalo August 15 Basque celebration, 1991. Source: Johnson County Library, Basque Photos collection.

Dollie Iberlin

I was born in Sheridan, Wyoming and have lived in Johnson County most of my life. Still, I wasn't really aware of the Basque community until I married Simon Iberlin. I developed a great fondness for the Basque people whose social gatherings reminded me of the German-Russian get togethers I went to as a child where all the generations met to eat, visit, and dance. Only with the Basque people you also heard singing.

My favorite Wyoming place is our ranch, Four Mile. I love the big birds and game, and the gumbo lilies in springtime. The three-room cabin, never modernized, is the same as it was fifty years ago when Amatxi, the Iberlin matriarch, furnished it. It's efficient and I treasure its unpretentiousness. Kind of like the Basque people I know.

I maintain an art studio in Buffalo, and I've been lucky enough to travel to and paint in the Pyrenees. My work includes many subjects including sheep and sheep wagons. In the past few years, I've discovered painting furniture and now work regularly on what I call the Old Master Series—straight-backed wooden chairs covered with paintings reminiscent of classic works of European art—Renoir, Monet, Gauguin, and others.

Powder River to the Bighorns

Buffalo, Wyoming, 1902. Jean Esponda straightened his shoulders, squinted his dark eyes approvingly at the Big Horn Mountains, and stepped off the train. Beside him was his new employer, Mr. Patsy Healy. When Healy hired Esponda, a web began to spin which eventually covered the land from the Big Horns to Powder River in Johnson County, Wyoming with a unique race of people.

Many Basque people followed Jean Esponda. They, too, stood staring at the same seemingly endless land, feeling anticipation and perhaps an edge of fear. Johnson County was a long way from their homeland's hills and white houses.

After seventeen years in California sheep production, Jean could see that the open range would soon be a thing of the past. He sold his California holdings and went back to the Pyrenees for a six-month visit. Returning to America, he met Patsy Healy on a westbound train from Chicago. The two men's conversation focused on sheep as the train rolled on across Union Pacific country then north through Burlington country and into Wyoming. They passed Gillette and at Clearmont got off the train to continue on the last twenty-eight miles to Buffalo by stagecoach. By the time the two men got to town, Jean was a new employee on the Johnson County ranch of Healy and Patterson, the largest sheep ranch in northeastern Wyoming.

Jean attracted his brother John to Healy and Patterson, and soon the Basques began coming to Johnson County. Brother met brother and cousin met cousin as the stagecoach came into town.

Many of the new immigrants started their flocks by taking sheep in lieu of wages. Often two Basques would become partners. One would stay with the sheep wagon and the sheep on the open range while the other would work as camp tender, bringing groceries and supplies from town. As sheep numbers increased, and as herders married, many partnerships were dissolved and Basques became individual ranch owners.

Sheep wagons provided housing for many of the first Basque couples. One new bride said, "What is this? In Europe we have houses to live in."

The sheep wagon, a specialized descendant of the Conestoga, came equipped with a built-in three-quarter size bed, a drop-down table, a bench on each side of the table with storage underneath, and a small wood or coal burning stove. A barrel placed next to the wagon, or a nearby spring provided water. In winter, sheep pelts, salted down and scraped, covered the floor and benches in wall-to-wall wool.

These were humble beginnings, but the Basque people put great emphasis on physical endurance, and short-range comforts were not considered, only the long-range goal of acquiring sheep and land.

As the individual Basque's sheep and land holdings increased, so did his bank account and his self-confidence. One of the early immigrants, Simon Harriet, at a point in his life when he was the largest landowner in the county, said to a mascaraed lady sitting on the bar stool next to him at the American Legion Club, "I am verry, verry rich, and verry verry good-looking and—ahhh, would you have loved me when I was sixty!" Well spoken for an eighty year old sipping his whiskey, but the "verry verry rich" future looked doubtful when he first came to America.

After the long ocean voyage to America, and the train ride so many other Basques had taken west, Simon Harriet stepped down in Clearmont and took the stagecoach the last twenty-eight miles to Buffalo. It was February and Simon, wearing canvas shoes, occasionally got down from the stage and ran beside it in an attempt to warm his feet.

At last the stage stopped in front of the Occidental Hotel on Buffalo's Main Street. Not one solacing ray of sunshine gleamed, not a welcoming word or glance greeted him from the people he saw. When he heard the stagecoach's wheels receding behind him, he felt panic and turned, running to catch the stage, prepared to go anywhere it was going rather than remain in Buffalo. But Simon ran in vain as the stage outdistanced him. Defeated and still cold, he turned again and walked slowly back to the Occidental to wait for his brother Peter.

As a herder for Healy and Patterson, Simon was aware of what was called the "deadline," a deep furrow cattlemen had plowed to mark the limit of where sheep were "allowed" to graze. Sheep were to remain south of the line. Simon had long been tempted to cross the deadline in search of new grazing ground. One morning, he gave in to his temptation. He took his personal belongings and food out of his sheep wagon and cached these in case his wagon was pushed over or burned before his return. That evening when Simon returned, he was relieved to find the sheep wagon undamaged. Emboldened, Simon continued to graze his sheep in forbidden territory. Eventually, the plowed furrow lost its authority completely when Simon and his partner, Bernard Marton, marched their bands of sheep across the deadline and made the new land another part of their personal domain.

Simon and Bernard were among the first Basques who helped to build a large and important Basque sheep industry in Johnson County. In 1932, the *Buffalo Bulletin* reported that, "The French (Basque) wool pool, one of the largest pools in the west, comprising 102,010 fleeces, has been seeking bids this week from various buyers."

In the early days all sheep were sheared at the Double Crossing pens near Clearmont. The greasy wool, filled with lanolin, was stomped into large bags, tied up and put on wagons to begin its long journey to the woolen mills in the East. Later other shearing pens were built and, finally, with improved roads and vehicles, shearing crews were able to come to each ranch. Often these were Australian crews who brought their portable shearing plants and pens to handle the sheep.

After shearing, the herder trailed his sheep to the Big Horn Mountains. Scars, still visible on the north slope of Crazy Woman Hill, are a testimony to the many sheep that passed along that trail.

In summer several hundred thousand sheep streamed onto the flower-covered slopes of the Big Horn Mountains. Basque herders from Buffalo mingled with their Scottish and Irish counterparts from Natrona County, and with Mormons from the Bighorn Basin. Although there was always a lot of work, there was also a flourishing summer social scene. Sheep wagons dotted the landscape and other "establishments," too, appeared. Shankersville and Cheevers Flat boasted girls and dancehalls. Cheevers Flat was ultimately burned down by the Irish bosses from Natrona County.

"Lightning came in the form of Pat Sullivan," people said.

Once, a thick fog enveloped the mountains. Three days later, when the fog lifted, the party-weary sheepherders stumbled out of their wagons to find eighteen thousand sheep mixed together. Groaning, the herders began the formidable task of sorting sheep. After another three days—this time of whistling, whooping, and shouting, the job was done. The herders had their sheep back and returned to their wagons to tend to their business.

The life of a sheepherder was lonely. Besides suffering from isolation, new herders anxiously watched the large bands of sheep that often traversed many miles. A new herder was acutely aware of the importance of keeping his sheep separate from neighboring sheep. The use of sheepdogs was a new experience, and the threat of predators, usually in the form of coyotes, was constant.

Herders used a variety of tactics to discourage coyotes. Scarecrows, flapping away in the herder's old clothes, would fool a coyote for a while. Sometimes, after the sheep were bedded down for the night, the herder would drag a kerosene-soaked rag around the band to keep coyotes away. A herder might also build a fire around the resting sheep. During World War II, bullets were impossible to buy in Buffalo and so firecrackers replaced the gunshots that had formerly been used to scare away coyotes.

One summer night Bernard Marton awakened to barking dogs and milling sheep. Bernard grabbed his rifle and shot at a moving object, which fell. When he reached the dead animal, Bernard was surprised to find that he'd killed a wolf. In the fall, he took the wolf pelt by horseback to Worland, Wyoming where he collected the two hundred dollar bounty. That was a lot of money in 1920. Local Basque people long believed that the wolf Bernard killed was the last one to live in the Big Horns.

All summer, herders looked forward to August fifteenth when the Basque people in the county gathered at Esponda's summer headquarters at Hazelton. Here, the Basques celebrated the Feast of the Assumption. A Basque missionary priest heard confessions and recited the Mass. As the herders knelt on the cool grassy ground, they were both grateful to fulfill their religious duties, and happily anticipating the coming dinner and dancing.

Soon after dinner, Santiago Michelena or Frank Aretcha's accordion resounded a sharp chord and a fast waltz began. The rousing sound of familiar music and the red wine served at dinner intensified the athletic young Basque men's need to celebrate.

Leaping up, a herder would pierce the air with a long *irrintzi*, the throaty yodel-like call that was a signal of the young man's joy. Hands high, fingers snapping, he would then begin to dance. Turning quick circles, his eye might catch the eye of an American girl, and he might extend his hand to her, palm upward, as an invitation to dance.

"You come to play with the Basque?"

The young woman might hesitate.

"You play," he'd say, then cinch her waist with a firm hand, and the two would begin to circle the floor.

Later, as the Basque women put away the food, the young herders would continue to drink and dance. These single men paid for the liquor for the party and the accordion player was paid by passing the hat. The next morning a herder might not remember how he'd gotten back to his wagon, but he welcomed his hangover as a sign of a dance well danced, and a party well partied. He then was content to finish the summer's herding in relative solitude.

There are other events, not as pleasant as the August fifteenth celebration and party, that stand as landmarks in the lives of Johnson County's Basque people. One of these took place during Easter week of 1973. On Ash Wednesday, a light snow began which was welcomed for the much-needed moisture it would bring. Soon the flakes got smaller and picked up speed as they slanted with the wind. The swirling snow blotted out the landscape.

Brothers John and Simon Iberlin felt their cabin fever increase as the visibility from the ranch house decreased. The snow gradually filled the space between the windows and the screens and the blizzard held them captive in the house. Two days and three nights later, the wind stopped and the two brothers shoveled their way out into a quiet white world.

They started the recalcitrant Caterpillar bulldozer and with it shoved the snow aside to reach the barn and sheds. After tending twenty-five heifers in the barn, they anxiously began to look for livestock that had been outside. Many sheep could still be alive under the snowdrifts.

Two days later, Simon and John were out searching on horseback. Simon spotted a solitary dark spot on a white slope. The two riders worked their way toward the puzzling object that turned out to be a bull's head. The bull's massive body was buried under the snow so that he was unable to move. His mournful eyes and snow-blasted patent leather cheeks attested to his suffering. Using an old fence post as a shovel, the men dug the bull out of his cold trap. It was a slow trip back to the corrals as the bull could only walk on his ankle bones. Still, the bull was lucky; he survived. In one draw Simon and John found a pile of dead bucks, and as the snow melted more and more dead sheep were uncovered—six hundred in all. It was a common story which repeated itself in early May 1984.

Though a blizzard during lambing or shearing time is especially dangerous, a heavy wet snow can kill a wooly sheep as well as a sheared one. As the sheep's wool fills with snow, it becomes so heavy that the sheep, exhausted, lies down, is buried in snow, and dies.

In addition to the uncertainties of weather and predation loss, sheep ranchers face fluctuating market prices for their products. The periods in which Basque ranchers were able to buy land in Johnson County coincided with good prices for both lamb and wool. Between 1941 and 1950, when prices were generally good, the Basques acquired over a hundred thousand acres of Johnson County land.

Prices go up and down. Management practices change. Old Simon Harriet (to distinguish him from Tall Simon and Just-Plain-Simon) shook his head in disapproval as his son spent ten cents a hole to put posts in the ground and build a fence.

"Younger people think a fence will do their work." Old Simon said.

Now solar wells, electric fences, cellular phones, Spot One (to replace dusting with insecticide for ticks), guard dogs, and llamas have all become "tools of the trade." Each generation is aware of innovations in ranch practices. Each generation applies new techniques.

The sheep themselves and overcoming the hardships that came with raising sheep were the first priorities in the lives of the first Basque people to come to Johnson County. Other parts of life— romance, marriage, family, and socializing—all had to fit into the schedules of other people or events. There were nature's sudden storms, the delayed arrival of a shearing crew, changing dates for shipping, a cold snap that demanded postponing lambing and docking. For all of these, the rancher had to be prepared.

At least partly as a result of factors such as these, many of Buffalo's Basque couples married later than their American counterparts. These Basque families were usually small. Other factors that influenced Basque family patterns in the early days included World War I, which interrupted many romances in the Pyrenees, and the simple fact of immigration itself, which demanded much time in adjusting physically and emotionally to life in the new country.

When Basque couples finally did marry, work continued to dominate their lives. Basque women did not expect praise from their husbands. Neither did they expect gifts or flattery. A man and a woman were partners in a dual adventure that required hard work and faith in one another. Men were not knights in shining armor; they were sheepherders struggling to own their own ranches.

Whether as herder or owner, husband or wife, the Basque's life was governed by the yearly cycles of working sheep. Money came in twice a year, and people had to budget and plan accordingly. One difficult period could mean great hardship for the entire family.

However arduous practical duties could be, the Basque people's lives were made rich by love and laughter, by an understanding of the ways of the land, and by a commitment to community solidarity that helped many a Basque survive hard times and prosper again. The heritage of the Basque people in Johnson County, the heritage that began over a hundred years ago with Jean Esponda's serendipitous journey to Buffalo, continues to live in this community. May it live far into the future.

A Sheepman

Simon Iberlin was a thirty-eight-year-old sheep rancher with thick black hair that curled forward. His nose had a slight right hook, and when he smiled one front tooth sported a silver edge. I was a widow with two young children. My best friend set us up on a date and we went to dinner. When the band started to play, he asked me to dance. I stepped into his robust arms, and he danced so smoothly and effortlessly that I never wanted to stop.

Summer Saturday nights turned into parties, and afterward, late at night, Simon would drive up the Big Horn Mountains to check on his sheep camp. The next day he'd come down the mountain and drive fifty miles east on gravel roads to see his brother John on their Wormwood ranch.

After I'd dated Simon for several weeks, he and his cousin Art Esponda, along with both men's mothers, took a sixty-day agricultural tour of South America. When Simon returned he proposed.

We set the date for our wedding, and then Simon changed it. Later, he changed it again. Each change put the wedding off for a week or so. I understood he wasn't wavering. It was just that our September marriage ceremony butted up against the fall work of gathering and shipping the sheep. We finally went ahead and married in the midst of the fall work. But the work was always there and in the coming years we never celebrated our anniversary. It came and went without our attention and, in the end, we forgot the exact date.

Before we married Simon lived with his mother in a modest white house on Burritt Street. He was dedicated to his sheep and most days he commuted to the Iberlin Four Mile Ranch. He drove

Jeeps and Fords, heavy duty vehicles loaded with supplies and tools. The trip ended with thirteen miles up and down two-track gravel and dirt roads. The solitary ranch had a shearing shed, a barn, a tool and machine shop, and a two-room cabin. The cabin was a Spartan place whose only amenities were a propane stove and refrigerator. There was no running water though outside there was a cistern full of rainwater. There was also a woodpile and an outhouse.

After a day in the country, Simon liked to stop at the 21 Club, a bar where the Basques gathered. It was an information hub—who was on trail, how many lambs were docked, when the sheep shearers were coming, what was the price of wool and lamb, who had sheep dogs. Simon always had a border collie in the back of his pickup, and after he married me, he took my dachshund along, too. At the bar, the sheep dog would stay in the pickup, but the dachshund would jump out and wait at the bar's front door. If I drove down Main Street and saw my dog in front of the bar, I knew Simon was almost home. I never went in. Simon's aunt, Mrs. Harriet told me, "Don't worry, when he's hungry he'll come home."

Simon grew up in a household and neighborhood of people who spoke Basque. His aunt and uncle, Catherine and Simon Harriet, along with their three boys, lived across the alley. The Irigarays lived nearby, too. As a first grader, Simon didn't speak English and so depended on his friend Mary Irigaray to translate the schoolwork.

When he was nine, Simon lived with his Uncle Pete Etchemendy in the Big Horn Mountains. His lessons were fishing, herding, and cooking. Uncle Pete rose early, built a fire in the sheep wagon stove, and went out to check his sheep, letting Simon stay in bed. Through the years Simon slept in many sheep wagons, and a couple times he slept under a wagon, once because the herder was too smelly and once because the herder was entertaining a lady friend.

In high school Simon played football and basketball with his Basque buddies Pete Camino, Putchie Harriet, and Charles Marton. In his senior year he had a date to the prom with the attractive daughter of a non-Basque cattle rancher. Simon rode on horseback from his father's Four Mile Ranch into town for the prom. When he arrived, he learned that his date and several other young couples had been invited to another cattleman's home for a pre-prom dinner. This cattleman had given Simon's father John his first job in America—sheepherding. Now Simon was the only of the young people who hadn't been invited to the dinner.

If not good enough for the cattleman, he was good enough for at least one of the Basque ranchers who offered Simon ten thousand dollars to marry the man's daughter. It was a lot of money but Simon turned down the offer. He said that he always felt affection for the old man who wanted to keep the Basque lineage going in his family.

Once I asked Simon why he waited until he was almost forty years old before getting married. He said, "I would have a date and then go to the country for a couple weeks and when I'd get back the girl would be going with someone else." He also thought he didn't have enough money to get married because he and his brother John were in debt.

As young men the boys worked with their father on the Four Mile Ranch. As they expanded their sheep numbers, they had to lease more land. Eventually they needed to buy another place. They'd heard about the Wormwood ranch, east of Four Mile but still in the Powder River Basin country. Other Basque ranchers—Esponda, Harriet, Camino, Etchemendy, Irigarary, Falxa, Michelena, Marton, Curuchet, and Urruty—all ran sheep in the basin.

Simon took his uncle Simon Harriet—known as Old Simon—along to visit Wormwood. Most of the land they traveled across that day belonged to Old Simon, a man who'd come to Wyoming from the village of Arnegi in the French Basque Country, who'd never learned to read or write, and yet who'd amassed over ninety thousand acres. Old Simon liked the looks of the Wormwood place and so did Simon and his brother John. They made an offer that was accepted then were sent reeling when the bank told them it had denied their loan.

Through a friend they spoke to an agent of the Kansas City Life Insurance Company who said he wanted to see the livestock water. Simon drove him to every windmill, creek, and reservoir on both the Wormwood and Four Mile Ranches and the Iberlins got their twenty-year loan.

Simon's brother John and his wife Maggie moved to Wormwood and Simon put two-way radios in the pickups for communication. One day as he stood leaning halfway in the window of his Jeep to talk with his brother John on the radio, lightning struck the roof and Simon flew backwards landing on the rocky road. A sheepherder ran over and leaned down over the unconscious body. When Simon finally sat up, the herder said, "I thought you dead."

There were plenty of other accidents. Once, when Simon and I were working in a corral, a dally I had on my saddle horn slipped, and the edgy horse Simon was on came unhinged, slamming Simon into the corral fence. Another time, Trouble, a crafty horse, stopped so fast that Simon was thrown into the air. When he came back down—landing in the saddle—he cracked his pelvis. This happened two days before the North American Basque Organization's national festival, which Buffalo was hosting for the first time. Simon, the festival chairman, attended the event on crutches.

While teaching the kids to drive, Simon also taught the lessons of life: "Never pass a windmill without checking on it." "Vice grips are the world's best invention." "French Basques are lovers, Spanish Basques are fighters." "Always get along with your neighbor." To his son and nephews: "Never have a gate that your wife can't open." And to his daughters and nieces: "It's just as easy to love a rich man as a poor one."

Our neighbors were all Basque ranchers. Harriet's land paralleled Four Mile on the north and east. So when Old Simon Harriet's estate was to be sold Simon gathered a group including his brother, two nephews, a cousin, and the cousin's son to discuss buying some of the Harriet land. A nephew said, "How do you buy a ranch?" And Simon answered, "You borrow money and pay it back for twenty years."

The huge property was to be sold in eleven parcels. Several meetings later, each person had selected a parcel of land to bid on and they'd agreed not to bid against each other. The sale day came. A prospective buyer had to put down ten thousand dollars in order to place a bid. Rumors were flying that Ted Turner, the Nature Conservancy, or some grazing association would swoop in and buy all the

Harriet land, but the auction crowd included mainly familiar men in cowboy hats or in caps advertising local stores.

After four rounds of bidding, with breaks in between, Simon's group had bought the entire ranch for nearly 4 million dollars. They met immediately after the sale to divide it up. Later they were sued by a disgruntled rancher who called the group "The Basque cartel." The word "mafia" was also used. The judge ruled in favor of the "cartel" and Simon took out another twenty-year loan. He was seventy years old.

By now Simon and I had adopted two of our grandsons and the pickup was again a driver's training vehicle. With Simon now over seventy, the pickup's jockey box was filled with inhalers, cough drops, and face masks. After years of smoking Camel cigarettes, dusting sheep with tick dust, and spraying thistles and other noxious weeds with herbicides, his lungs began to slacken. On winter mornings, he tied a bandana around his nose and mouth to keep out the cold. Still, the work and the boys were reasons to get up every day. And, to those of us who knew Simon as a rancher, husband, father, and friend, it seemed he could take anything.

Then, when the grandsons graduated from high school, Simon began to fail. One day he stood in front of his fifty silk ties, sleek and waiting to be worn, and tried to remember how to knot one. Now and then he would forget a word and finally he ignored traffic lights. He'd always loved a good meal but now he lost his sense of smell, which meant he lost his sense of taste. Still, he enjoyed his food, saying, "I eat by memory." There were other memories—as he slept he spoke aloud in Basque and he remembered his dreams. They were always about sheep and horses, and he would wake up disturbed, thinking the dreams were real and wondering why he was in bed.

One evening as I was driving him home from a restaurant, he said, "May I ask you a question?"

"Yes." I said.

"What is your name?"

Simon died late in the afternoon on the last day of 2010. He had been a county commissioner, a state highway commissioner, a director of three banks and the local hospital. He was a World War II veteran and proud of his navy service. And through it all, under that Pendleton shirt over that big chest, beat the heart of a sheepman.

Irigaray sheep camp near Powder River east of Buffalo, Wyoming, early 1920s. Source: Johnson County Library, Basque Photos collection.

Frances Beckner Thompson

In the mid 1950s, I came from Indiana to Buffalo, Wyoming where I went to work as a registered nurse in the local hospital. Brought here initially by my love of mountains and wide open spaces, I quickly developed an affinity also for the good people of this land, among whose numbers were Catherine Marton and Jean Auzqui, of whom I've written.

An avid hiker, backpacker, and amateur photographer, I have experienced the beauty of this area as few take the opportunity to do. For this reason especially, I enjoy sharing my experiences with friends through slide shows and personally conducted day trips.

Retired now from nursing, I can visit my favorite haunts more often and, perhaps, write more stories about the dear folk of Johnson County.

Against All Odds

On Friday afternoon, November 15, 1957, I helped a Basque sheep-herder with a broken leg out of a pickup and into the hospital in Buf-falo, Wyoming. He was Jean Auzqui. His horse had fallen on him four days before. Jean had then crawled three-quarters of a mile through sagebrush, cactus, and snow to his sheep wagon and waited there alone, day after day, until the camp tender found him and brought him to town.

As I laid him on the X-ray table and began to unwrap the crude splint of dishtowels and table knives, I apologized for having to move him. He placed his hand lightly on my arm and said in his broken accent, "Oh, Missy, nothing you do hurts like what I been through."

Jean, or Cashau as his friends called him, had worked for the Esponda Ranch for ten years and was one of the ranch's most val-ued employees. He was a loner, a bachelor, and sheepherding was his daily way of life. On the Monday he'd broken his leg, he was camped in Powder River country about twenty-five miles east of town. The camp tender had been out that forenoon and helped him move his wagon and sheep to a new location, and then left him to his solitary life.

Around noon Jean rode off to check the sheep. As he crossed a reservoir, his horse slipped on ice, threw him to the ground, and fell on top of his left leg. The horse wasn't hurt, but Jean had a shattered leg. He tried to call the horse to him, but she wouldn't come close enough to let him grab the reins. Realizing that he must get to the wagon, or die of exposure, he started crawling. Up and down hill he snaked around sagebrush and cactus, slithered through patches of snow, and scraped over rocks, dragging his painful leg, inch by inch.

Seven hours passed and night had fallen before he covered the three-quarters of a mile to the wagon.

He was exhausted when he got to the wagon and it was only with great difficulty that he climbed up and pulled himself through the door. When he got inside, he collapsed and spent the night on the floor where he lay moaning through a sleepless night.

On Tuesday he looked out across two miles of open country to a dirt road. Cars occasionally passed but none stopped. A neighboring rancher drove by, glanced toward Jean's camp, saw the wagon with smoke coming from the chimney, and assumed that all was well.

Some men wouldn't have had the courage to stay put. In desperation, they might have tried to cross the two miles. Jean thought calmly about what to do. He might be able to crawl to the road, but he might not. On the other hand, he knew that, though it might be several days or weeks before anyone found him in the wagon, eventually someone would come if he stayed where he was. So he waited.

He was used to solitude and was a self-sufficient person, but now he faced an ordeal of survival. It was early winter and he had a crippling injury. The cards, as they say, were stacked against him.

He bound his leg in layers of dishtowels, using a butcher knife and tableware as splints. He folded a blanket into a kind of sling to support his leg while he crawled outside for wood and water. He knew he had to keep a fire going and he knew that a person can survive a long time on water alone.

On Wednesday his swollen leg throbbed with unrelieved agony, but he had to bring in more wood and water. A layer of ice covered the water barrel so he scooped up a panful of snow and set it on the stove to melt. For nourishment, he added sugar to the water and drank the mixture. Wednesday passed; no one came.

Thursday was his fifty-sixth birthday. He wondered if he'd live to see his fifty-seventh. He wondered how long he could last. He asked himself, "What if no one comes?" He watched the slow hours move on. Thursday, too, ended and no one came.

On Friday morning about eleven, he saw a pickup turn off the dirt road and head toward his wagon. Relief flooded through him.

Shortly after, Jean Errecart lifted the weakened sheepherder into the car and brought him over the rough roads to Buffalo where gentle hands and food and medicine awaited him.

I offered to bring Jean in from the pickup on a stretcher, but he waved me aside, threw his blanket sling under his foot and slid sideways into a wheelchair, saying, "I come all the way sitting up; I sit up now."

The doctors feared he would lose his leg. When we unwrapped it, we found a black, swollen mass from which hung large blood blisters. Some of these broke as the towels came off, and a reddish-orange liquid spilled out.

X-rays showed multiple fractures of both bones in his lower leg with splintered fragments of bone jutting out at odd angles. Treatment began with narcotics, intravenous feedings, antibiotics, shots for tetanus and gas gangrene, a blood transfusion, and food. We placed a cradle over the bed to keep the blankets off his leg. Five days later, the doctors put a pin through his heel and applied traction to the leg. Then they waited for time and nature to work their miracles.

Jean was in a fracture bed strung with ropes and pulleys and an overhead monkey bar by which he could raise himself and shift positions slightly. He occasionally needed a shot for what he described as "jumping pains." He rarely rang for a nurse and, when he did, he apologized for asking for help. That he needed help seemed to give him more pain than his leg.

Weeks dragged by. Jean had few diversions—he didn't know how to read, he had no family to visit him, he was uninterested in either television or radio, and he had no hobbies to occupy his hands. A few friends stopped by to see him but mostly he lay quietly. He had no need to keep busy and never seemed restless. He seemed to me to be an island, self-contained. The quiet months in the hospital were in some ways no different than the long silences in the sheep wagon. Those of us who cared for him fretted about ways to help him fill the long days. We seemed unable to accept that he was content. It was we who were not.

After two months, X-rays showed the beginning of new bone growth and Jean graduated to a plaster cast and a wheelchair. Three days later, I handed him a pair of crutches. He beamed at me and slid out of bed to stand upright. He was awkward at first and top heavy, but soon he had the knack of walking one-legged and thereafter his bed was empty except at night.

A week later the doctors discharged him and I said goodbye to this quiet, smiling man as he swung out of the hospital door with the vigor of a man returning to life. He stayed in town for the several months until the cast came off, and then returned to his beloved sheep wagon.

After he left the hospital, I learned that Jean liked to gamble. I think he must have been very good at it because, at least once, he had gambled, against all odds, for his life, and won.

I saw Jean only once more after that. It was the following summer. He was stomping along the streets of downtown Buffalo, as good as new. He didn't even limp, and his friends said that he never once complained of his leg aching.

Jean continued to work for the Esponda family until his death of an apparent heart attack many years later. His body was found in a pasture where he'd gone to check sheep.

Wyoming's Mother of the Basques

The first time I saw Mrs. Marton she stood framed in the doorway of a sheep wagon, her dark eyes snapping with pleasure, her sensitive face open in friendship to this stranger who had arrived at suppertime without an invitation. The glow she radiated contrasted sharply with her somber attire, for she wore the black clothes of a woman in mourning. But there was no sign of grief in her greeting. Arms widespread, she gathered me in a maternal embrace, saying, "Hallo, hallo! You're just in time for supper. I fix you a place."

I sat down to a tiny, sliding shelf of a table set with enameled tin plates. Around the table crowded her sons and sheepherders, suddenly timid at my female invasion. The men made shy repartee in Basque, nodded meaningfully in my direction and then burst out laughing. I joined in the laughter though I knew I was the butt of a joke.

Then silence fell. In her brusque yet tender way, Mrs. Marton scolded the swarthy men and, turning to me, said, "Chilo and them boys all the time saying they want girls—where are the girls—and then you come and they got girls, and they not say a word. Chilo, he dumb, he not say anything."

Grinning broadly at their embarrassment, she set before us man-sized portions of mutton stew, and handed over a loaf of homemade bread that each in turn broke a chunk from as we settled down to one of the finest meals I've ever had. The *chahakoa*, a wine bag lined with goat hair, was passed around, for no Basque meal is complete without wine. The experienced tipped the *chahakoa* up to arc a stream of red liquid into their mouths, never spilling a drop.

Enchanted by the homey atmosphere inside the sheep wagon and by the low bleating of sheep as they bedded down in the sage-covered hills outside, I wondered what manner of woman this was who held the reins of ranch and men so gently in her hands; who brought such boisterous, raw-boned sons to quiet attention; who wore a dress of sorrow but a countenance of joy; who made a stranger feel like one of the family; and who evoked the respect due a matriarch. I didn't know then that as the years passed I'd come to know and love this woman who was mother to young and old, friend to rich and poor, and inspiration to all who opened their hearts to her.

Catherine Iriart was born June 21, 1897 in Baigorri, a small town in the Basque Pyrenees, in what is now France. She lived with her parents, four sisters, and two brothers in a rock house, cemented over and whitewashed. She walked a mile to a Catholic school where she graduated at the age of twelve. Because there was no high school in Baigorri this ended her formal education. When her brothers were killed in World War I, the five girls had to manage the farm. Those years of hard work, together with the independence that grew out of a sense of responsibility, gave Catherine a solid base on which to build her future.

At twenty-three, she came to the United States at the insistence of her older sister Grace who had preceded her to Wyoming, and with the help of a cousin, Mrs. Pete Harriet, who paid her passage. A picture of young Catherine, taken the day after her arrival in Buffalo, shows she had smooth skin, full lips, and a stubborn chin all under a head of black hair. A kind of purity radiated from her face—a purity that, half a century later, still set her apart as a good woman in the noblest sense.

She worked for the Baker family whose daughter, Charlotte, told me, "Mrs. Marton taught us French and we taught her English. She used to say, 'Damned fool oven won't work,' or 'Damned fool cake won't bake.' I think those were the first English words she learned— 'damned fool.'"

While working for the Bakers, Catherine Iriart met Bernard Marton, a young sheep rancher who was born in Arnegi, across the river from the Iriarts. "I knew his sister in the Old Country," said Mrs. Marton.

Bernard proposed and she accepted, but the Bakers had house-guests and she didn't want to leave them in the lurch. Charlotte remembered that, "Rather than leave my parents without help at a time when they particularly needed it, she made Bernard wait."

They were married on November 14, 1923, when she was twenty-six and he twenty-nine. Their first home was a sheep wagon, their second, a house they shared with Grace and Gaston Irigaray, Mrs. Marton's sister and brother-in-law. Later, the Martons bought their house on Buffalo's North Main Street where she lived until her death, simply and proudly. She said, "My husband say one time, 'Never sell this house.' No, this is my home—I live here."

The house was also home to five children—Charles, John, James, Richard, and Bernadette. Richard drowned in Crazy Woman Creek at the age of one and a half. James was killed at twenty-nine in an automobile accident. The other three children and their families live in or near Buffalo.

When Charles and John were young, their parents homesteaded a section of land in the Scotch Corrals at the southern end of the Big Horn Mountains. They built a cabin, fences, and sheep corrals, and lived there during the summer for three years. When I asked Mrs. Marton about homesteading, she shrugged her shoulders and said, "What's to tell? It's just a bunch of men." I got much the same response when I told her I wanted to write about her. "What for? Why do you do that?" she asked. Perhaps really wonderful people don't recognize they're outstanding, because they live magnificently every day and, to them, it's natural and ordinary.

To find out about the homestead, I went to her sons and to a nephew, Domingo Martirena, who told me that the claims were about two miles apart and, in the summer, most of the Basque families went up there. Domingo told me suddenly they'd decide to go to somebody's cabin. They'd catch a bunch of fish, get some moonshine, and have a party. They'd dance all evening and half the night—often spend the night. They'd sleep all over the place. Then, they'd go home in the morning.

Every fall the Buffalo Basques made wine. Joe Sarantha, an Italian friend of the Martons, got grapes by the ton from California. The men, wearing rubber boots, crawled into large wooden barrels and stomped the grapes. The juice was then poured into fifty-gallon barrels, and the wine fermented for about two months. Sometimes, if grapes were hard to come by, wild chokecherries were used.

One summer when the Martons ran sheep at a place Lucy Sarantha called the Lee Cabin, they invited the Saranthas for a visit. Lucy said, "Catherine cooked such wonderful breakfasts of sourdough pancakes. You should have known her in those days. She was in Paradise with the family around her. You never got tired of being around Catherine. And Bernard—he was a very nice man, kindest of any I ever knew." Laughing, she added, "Bernard and I used to run foot races on the mountain. Oh, those were good days full of fun and laughter. We never talked of hard times."

Then in March 1947 tragedy hit. Bernard Marton had gone to Alliance, Nebraska with his sons Charles and James who were playing in a basketball tournament. During a game, Mr. Marton was stricken by a fatal heart attack. Mrs. Marton, at forty-nine, had four children ranging in age from eleven to twenty-three, and a twenty-five thousand acre ranch to run. Saddened beyond bearing, she seemed to die a little herself.

When we met ten years later her indomitable will had returned the light to her eyes and brought laughter back into her life. Only her black mourning dress remained as a token of her enormous grief. She never thought of selling the ranch and when I asked how she had managed, she said, "Oh, the boys were big enough." But her family tells another story, one that makes clear the devotion of an unselfish woman.

Each year in late April, Mrs. Marton went to the lambing camp to cook for six men who were caring for three thousand sheep. One of the men recalled that, "When she came, we had pies and cooking and laughter and fun. It was the only time of the year we had all that."

She lived in the sheep wagon and the men slept in tepees or under the open sky. First they would butcher a sheep or two for mutton or two which they ate twice a day—stewed, roasted, or in soup. Breakfasts were bacon or ham and eggs, and always there was homemade bread. Mrs. Marton baked every other day—the oven in a sheep wagon stove is small and six Basque men eat a lot of bread. It was the men's job to cut firewood, but often they were out with the sheep and so she chopped her own wood.

After a stout swig of whiskey and a cup of coffee, the men left each morning at four o'clock. At eight they returned, one or two at a time, for breakfast. Throughout the day, as they could, they ran in for a meal or a snack. She always had pie or pudding or coffee waiting. The only meal they ate together was at nine p.m. After that, she washed the dishes and went to bed for a few hours sleep before another dawn.

A camp tender came every ten days bringing supplies and fresh water. Two barrels of water had to last until the next visit. Sometimes Mrs. Marton saved wash water and used it over, lest they run out.

In the daily round of cooking, washing, and mending, she had little time for leisure. Still, she took whatever time she could to go walking over the land she loved—she never rode horseback.

The first aid kit was aspirin and Mercurochrome.[1] If one of the men became sick, she dosed him with hot milk and a slug of whiskey. Neither were there sanitation facilities—everybody took a turn in the draw.

In the spring of 1950, a severe snowstorm caught them at lambing time in Powder River country, thirty miles from the sheep sheds. Newborn lambs died by the hundreds. Even meadowlarks, stealing oats from under the sheep wagon, stayed there and froze to death.

---

1. A nineteenth-century product marketed for use on minor cuts and scrapes, it's reddish-brown color stained the skin when it was applied. The stain it left and its use of trace amounts of mercury led to its ban in the United States, although it is still widely used around the world. —eds.

To keep warm, the men set fire to dead trees along the river. If they had the good luck to find a wet lamb as it was born, they warmed it beside the fire before returning it to the ewe. Heartsick at seeing so many deaths, the men desperately tried to save the remaining unborn lambs by driving the herd fifteen miles in one day through snow toward Crazy Woman Creek.

Mrs. Marton walked most of the first four miles rather than risk the uncertain fate of sliding over mud and snow in a car. She especially disliked the mud, because a vehicle could so easily go out of control on it. Her daughter Bernadette recalls that at a muddy spot her mother would jump out of the car unless held down. Bernadette said, "I can hear James hollering, 'Git her in the middle,' as we came to a slick spot."

One might think that with so much hard work under difficult physical conditions and in all kinds of weather, Mrs. Marton might, as the years passed, have decided to stay in the comfort of her cozy house in town. She never thought of it. Work was healing and rewarding. She had her family—she needed them; they needed her. She lovingly gave of herself. And it is true that between hardship and heartache, there were times of gaiety.

Her niece Mary Lawrence remembers that, "Sometimes when my mother was away, I stayed with Amatxi (Basque for *Godmother*, and, in Buffalo, for *Grandmother*). Martons had an old Dodge and we'd put a dollar's worth of gas in it and take off. Once we ran out of gas in front of the Safeway. We got out and pushed the car through town, laughing hysterically."

Or, the only time Mrs. Marton drove, she loaded her five children along with the Irigaray children in a pickup truck and started for Saranthas. But not knowing how to stop the truck, she drove into a drainage ditch and up against a fence.

There was also the time she chased Domingo and James with a butcher knife. Mary Lawrence recalls that, "They got boozed up and were raising hell. She was cutting meat and she took after them with the butcher knife, calling out, 'Get out of here and go back to town.'"

Catherine Marton was a woman of great drive, full of the joy of living. She was also a woman of compassion. Over the years she cared for invalids and new mothers, she comforted the bereaved, nursed sick sheepherders back to health, and welcomed everyone to her house whether for a day or a week or a meal. She bought clothes for poor children at Christmas, gave food to friends and strangers, paid her nephew's passage to America, and entertained Basque boys after Mass on Christmas Eve when they came by the dozen and sat on her kitchen floor waiting for food. For countless Basque immigrants, she acted as interpreter in stores, banks, and at the hospital. A telephone call would bring her, just as she was, in her apron, to anyone's assistance.

In 1959, she suffered a severe stroke and lay for months in the hospital, partially paralyzed and sometimes unconscious. It was thought that she'd not recover enough to write or walk. Time and medicine and her will ruled otherwise.

After her recovery, she lived alone and justified it with the simple statement, "Why not? I sleep all night." During this part of her life she had a "bad" leg, but it carried her about the house and to the grocery store and, in 1961, back to the Basque country. She also had a "bad" arm, but it reached out to friends as warmly as ever. She had a "bad" hand, but it signed Christmas cards, wrote letters to her sister in Baigorri, and baked cookies for grandchildren.

Until her final illness, visitors still came and stayed with her, immigrant Basque boys still made her home one of their first stops in Buffalo, and strangers such as this one were still gathered into her maternal embrace.

Isidora Garro with infant Grace Esponda, around 1935, Buffalo, Wyoming.
Source: Johnson County Library, Basque Photos collection.

Playing leapfrog at August 15 Basque party in the Big Horn mountains, early 1920s.
Source: Johnson County Library, Basque Photos collection.

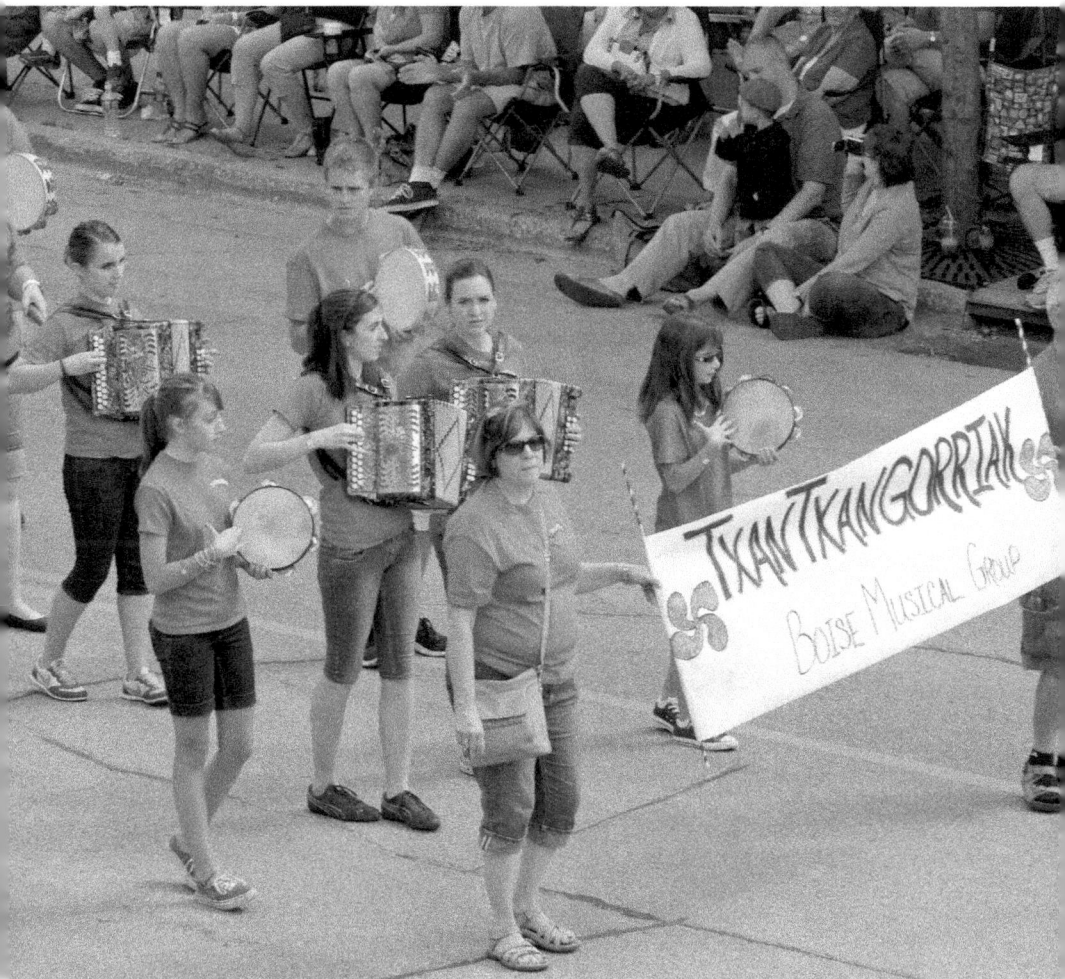

Boise, Idaho music group Txantxangorriak, NABO 2011, Buffalo, Wyoming.
Source: Photo by Tom Milsted, courtesy of *The Buffalo Bulletin*.

www.ingramcontent.com/pod-product-compliance
Lightning Source LLC
Chambersburg PA
CBHW070927270326
41927CB00011B/2759